VOLUME

1

FORECLOSURE PREVENTION

Loss Mitigation Specialist

Library of Congress -in-Publication Data
October 2009

Foreclosure Prevention – Loss Mitigation Specialist Basic Training

Printed in the United States of America

10 9 8 7 6 5 4 3 2 1

Coursework is available at special quantity discounts to use as premiums and sales promotions within corporate or private training programs. To obtain information or inquire about availability please write to Director, PO Box 1, Hollidaysburg, PA 16648.

FORECLOSURE PREVENTION

Loss Mitigation Specialist
Table of Contents

I

Introduction

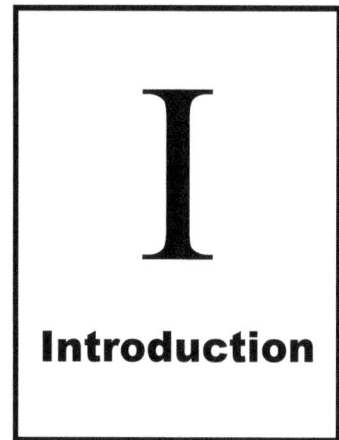

Congratulations on your decision to enter the field of loss mitigation or expand your current industry skill set to encompass the details of loss mitigation, loan modification, or refinance options.

Loss mitigation has long been an element within the banking industry. Present market conditions have caused this small segment of the industry to expand. This expansion presents you with an exceptional opportunity to enhance your career options. As a lender loss-mitigation expert, private loss-mitigation negotiator, or lender seeking career expansion through the processing of loss mitigation paper the newly expanded opportunity presented in loss mitigation specialization are unsurpassed in other, current career options.

You will use your newly learned skills to

- Streamline the negotiation process between homeowners and lending institutions

- Maximize the negotiation position for the party for whom you work

- Facilitate fair and timely resolution to financial crises

- Ensure all parties achieve the loss mitigation results best suited to the situation

- Scrutinize the qualifications inherent to each homeowner and property to ensure that all loss mitigation resolutions achieve long term sustainability

The position of a loss mitigation specialist provides you with the opportunity to become one of the respected professionals within your community.

➢ As a loss mitigation specialist who conducts their business based upon a solid foundation of knowledge and core best practices, you will gain the ability to choose the environment in which you wish to work.

You may choose to conduct your business from

Your home

In an office

Within a bank

Under the umbrella of a non-profit counseling agency

The skills you are obtaining are so prized within the lending community that you can gain the ability to obtain any position you set your sights on.

➢ You will receive an income that relates directly to how hard (or smart) you work.

The pay structure within the loss mitigation industry is based primarily upon the number of homeowners that you can assist with default work out plans. This structure enables you to expand your income to heights that are unattainable in other, similar career options!

➢ You will obtain the freedom available only through being the in charge of your career.

A loss mitigation specialist is one of the few individuals who have the ability to blend the respect of being an independent business professional with the security of working under the umbrella of a corporate environment and the flexibility of being in charge of their own business!

➢ You will have the opportunity to use your creativity and ingenuity to become the best in your chosen profession.

Loss mitigation guidelines are in place for each work out option that you will use during your career.

Each homeowner will have specific issues and situations within their lives that you must correlate to the correct loss mitigation workout.

Through the application of creative thinking and a comprehensive understanding of the loss mitigation options, you can blend the needs of the lender with the situation of the homeowner to create the perfect workout package for every default situation!

Research has shown that the most important attribute of a successful loss mitigation specialist is the drive to succeed within their chosen profession. The drive to succeed surpasses educational degrees, experience, and personal attributes. Purchasing this program shows that you have initial drive needed to begin on the path toward career stability and success and attain top-loss prevention negotiator status.

As a well-trained loss mitigation specialist, you may choose to follow a variety of career paths.

- Work within a lender's loss mitigation offices

  A loss mitigation specialist working on behalf of a lending institution works to negotiate the best possible transaction from the perspective of the lender.

- Work for a firm that handles the loss mitigation negotiations between the homeowner and the bank

  A loss mitigation specialist working on behalf of the homeowner through third-party contract or through a loss mitigation firm works to negotiate a transaction that will enable the homeowner to retain possession of the property. If this is not possible, the loss mitigation professional will attempt to negotiate a short sale position that enables the homeowner to sell the property without the lender requiring that they pay surplus funds out of their own pocket.

- Start your own business as a third party negotiator who facilitates negotiations between all of the interested parties in a loss mitigation negotiation. The homeowner, bank, investor, and real estate agents

    Negotiate a forbearance agreement between the parties that enables the homeowner to eliminate or reduce the monthly payment obligation until a temporary financial crisis has been rectified

    Negotiate a workable loan modification agreement that enable the homeowner to modify the existing home loan to a level that enables the homeowner to maintain the future payments while maintaining the value of the loan paper for the lender

    Negotiate and facilitate a new mortgage that will enable the homeowner to refinance their current note to a note that they can afford and avoid foreclosure.

    Negotiate the best possible short sale terms, or payoff acceptance, that enables the sale of the security property in the general real estate market at a minimal loss to the bank and with no excess amounts due from the homeowner.

    Negotiate a cash for keys transaction in which the lender will provide the homeowner with a specified amount of money in exchange for the homeowner relinquishing the property to the lender in good condition and in a timely manner. This minimizes the time requirements of a full foreclosure, maximizes the potential value of the property for the lender, and enables the homeowner to obtain a set amount of cash to find a new dwelling.

    Negotiate a deed in lieu of foreclosure where the bank halts the foreclosure process, enables the homeowner to provide the lender with the deed in exchange for a full satisfaction or release of the mortgage obligations of the homeowner from the lender

As a loss mitigation specialist, you will strive to negotiate the best possible transaction for the party you represent. The best possible transaction does not always correlate to the most profitable transaction. In loss mitigation negotiation, the best outcome is one that is sustainable and minimizes the likelihood of future default.

- You must gain an understanding of how each potential negotiation outcome will benefit and harm each party.

- You must become adept at negotiating each level of the loss mitigation process.

- You must gain the skills necessary to assess the financial condition of the homeowner and the value of the property to ensure that the loss mitigation resolution agreed to between the parties suits the specific situation of the file you are negotiating

- You must gain a comprehensive understanding of the flow or levels of loss mitigation negotiation to ensure that the lowest loss mitigation option necessary to cure the default is used in each situation

Over the coming weeks, this coursework will provide you with the foundation of knowledge, tools, and skills that you need to bring each transaction to the most successful conclusion possible.

It is important that you review each chapter within the course. Every element within the coursework builds on the information included within the other chapters. The companion skill-assessment workbook will enable you to complete self-test assessments. These assessments will provide you with insight into the areas of the text that may require additional reviews in order to gain the necessary skill set to succeed as a loss mitigation specialist.

The field of loss mitigation is an expanding arena that presents incredible opportunity for career expansion and growth. You will gain the ability to chart your own career path while ensuring that each day brings the satisfaction of knowing that your actions have increased the stability of the homeowner, the lender, and the national real estate market.

Loss Mitigation

The field of loss mitigation involves successfully negotiating a workout plan between a homeowner and a lender to cure a default situation.

The workout plan will enable the homeowner and the lender to mitigate the losses suffered when an unexpected occurrence make the maintenance of a previously negotiated mortgage loan impossible.

A loss mitigation specialist acts as a liaison to facilitate negotiations between a homeowner who is in or about to enter default status on a mortgage loan and the lender. The loss mitigation specialist will assist the parties in negotiating the most effective work out option to cure the default.

Loss mitigation negotiations opens up the possibility of multiple intervention techniques designed to prevent foreclosure. Each potential work out has specific negotiations, prerequisites and result for the involved parties.

When you are assisting in the loss mitigation negotiation, you should begin by screening to determine the least intervention necessary to cure the default situation. The final workout plan should assist in stabilizing the ability of the homeowner to retain the property.

If the homeowner or property makes the lesser level mitigation options impossible, then the higher-level options should be reviewed.

Gaining an understanding of the levels of negotiation available, the prerequisites, and effects of each will assist in streamlining the processes leading to a successfully negotiated transaction.

How it works:

1.   The homeowner has a personal situation, financial issue, or unforeseen alteration in circumstances that affect their ability to make payments on their mortgage.

2.   The homeowner falls behind on their mortgage 30, 60, or 90 days

3.   The loss mitigation department contacts the homeowner or the homeowner retains the services of a loss mitigation specialist

4.   The loss mitigation specialist completes a qualification package for the homeowner

5.   The loss mitigation specialist defines potential work out potions that may be available to the homeowner

6.   The homeowner reviews and approves the delinquency work out options

7.   The loss mitigation specialist prepares a negotiation package for the lowest level work out intervention

       The negotiation package is presented to both the lender and the homeowner

8.   The lender and the homeowner review the package contents and approve or decline the negotiation strategy

       Lender Decline   The lender decline of the negotiation strategy will typically contain optional work out offers or a counter offer

                                  Example: A homeowner instructs a retained loss mitigation specialist to present a short sale option when the lowest intervention level suitable for the homeowner's file would be a basic special forbearance to last a period of 4 months

The lender can decline the negotiation package in favor of a counter offer of the basic forbearance terms.

Most lenders will decline any loss mitigation offer that exceeds the lowest level necessary to promote payment stability for the homeowner. In this instance, the homeowner would appear to be a walk away or individual who is choosing to surrender the home rather than meet their obligations

If the lender presents a negotiation decline rather than a counter offer, the reason for the decline will be included in the formal notice. The homeowner may or may not be able to cure the reason for the lender decline.

Example: Lender decline – property is second home and does not meet the minimum qualification for loss mitigation negotiations

The homeowner would not be able to cure the basis of the lender decline and may wish to pursue other options such as a non-traditional sales venue

Homeowner Decline

Verifiable If the homeowner declines the lowest acceptable level of intervention, the reasons for the decline should be valid and verifiable.

Example: Homeowner discovers that the temporary job loss has become a permanent loss due to a company closure.

Employment opportunities in the homeowner's area are limited.

The previously negotiated and workable forbearance agreement is longer sustainable by the homeowner

The homeowner's decline of the negotiation plan is based on a fundamental change in circumstances. The loss mitigation specialist should review the new status of the homeowner to determine the next potential workout option available to meet the new needs of the homeowner.

Unverifiable If the homeowner decline is not for a verifiable cause, the loss mitigation negotiation will typically be halted. The purpose of the loss mitigation process is to assist homeowners in retaining possession of their homes. Any homeowner who has no desire to work with the loss mitigation team is a candidate for foreclosure rather than lesser mitigation efforts.

Example: The loss mitigation negotiations determine that the homeowner may resume making payments on the mortgage if the loan is re-amortized and a lower interest rate applies. These payments are sustainable and dictate enough surplus income to enable the homeowner to catch up the delinquent payments within 6 months.

The lender approves the loan modification terms.

The homeowner was seeking a walk away, or relinquishment of the property because they feel that values have fallen too drastically within their area for the property to be of value even under a loan modification term.

The homeowner has chosen not to participate at the lowest level intervention and the loss mitigation processes will end. The homeowner will be subject to the process of foreclosure.

9. **Acceptance**   If both parties agree with the negotiation package then the steps dictated by the mitigation option outlined within the presented plan are followed.

One of the fundamental functions of the loss mitigation professional is to negotiate a work out option that has the least impact on the parties involved. Loss mitigation options include a variety of work out stages. You should gain an understanding of the level of intervention applicable to each stage so that you can competently negotiate the most beneficial work out for the parties involved.

- The most beneficial workout for the lender may not be the work out option that increases the profitability of the plan. The stability, or homeowner's ability to maintain the work out agreement, is essential to a successful loss mitigation process.

- The most beneficial workout for the homeowner is not necessarily the one that is preferable to the homeowner. It is the work out plan that is sustainable and creates the least level of intervention.

You should gain an understanding of the levels of the loss mitigation tools available to you and the impact of each on the homeowner and the lender. It is essential that you negotiate the work out option that provides the lowest level of intervention while ensuring the maximum likelihood of default prevention.

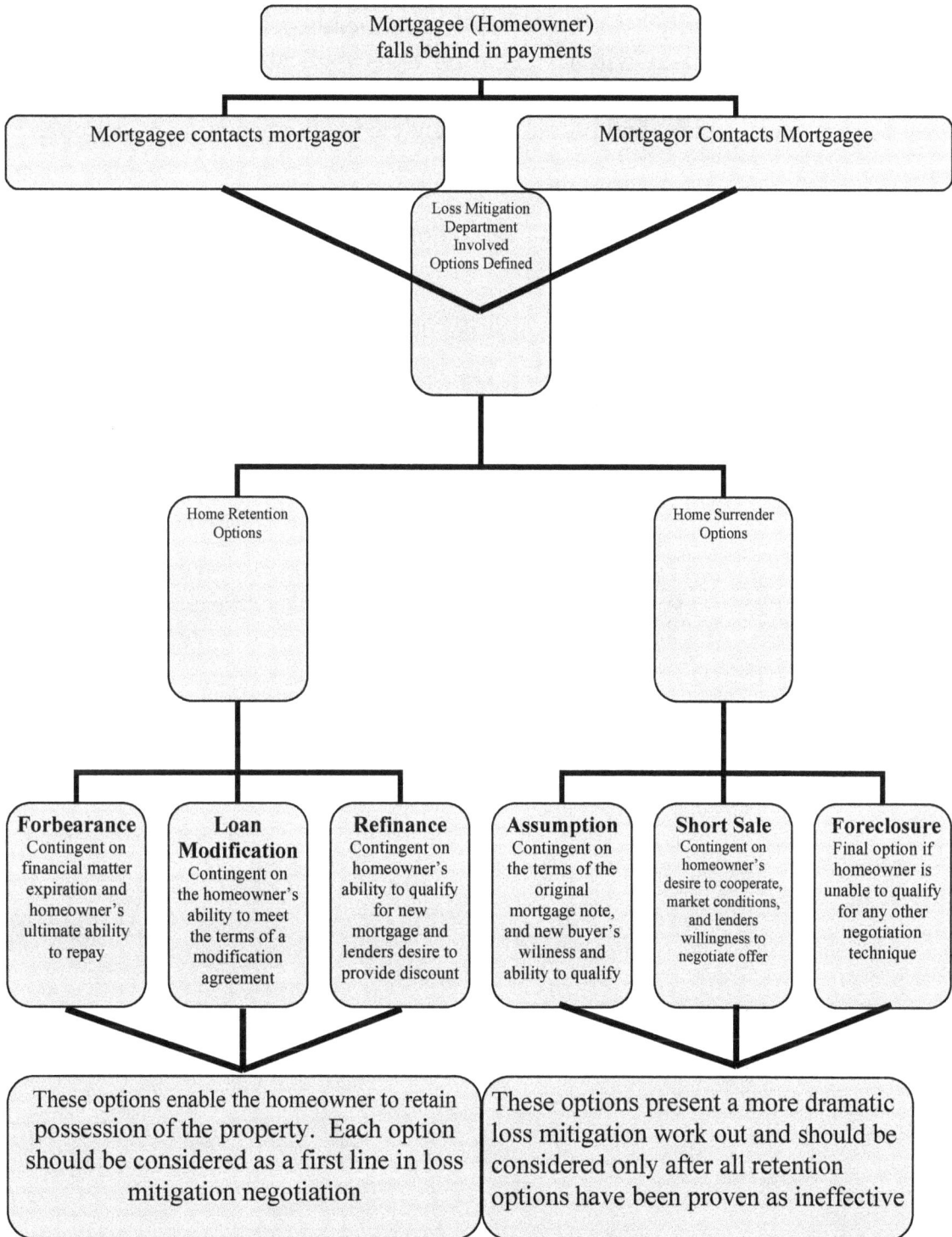

```
┌─────────────────────────────────────┐
│        Mortgagee (Homeowner)         │
│        falls behind in payments      │
└─────────────────────────────────────┘
```

Mortgagee contacts mortgagor	Mortgagor Contacts Mortgagee

Loss Mitigation Department Involved Options Defined

Home Retention Options

Home Surrender Options

Forbearance Contingent on financial matter expiration and homeowner's ultimate ability to repay	**Loan Modification** Contingent on the homeowner's ability to meet the terms of a modification agreement	**Refinance** Contingent on homeowner's ability to qualify for new mortgage and lenders desire to provide discount	**Assumption** Contingent on the terms of the original mortgage note, and new buyer's wiliness and ability to qualify	**Short Sale** Contingent on homeowner's desire to cooperate, market conditions, and lenders willingness to negotiate offer	**Foreclosure** Final option if homeowner is unable to qualify for any other negotiation technique

These options enable the homeowner to retain possession of the property. Each option should be considered as a first line in loss mitigation negotiation	These options present a more dramatic loss mitigation work out and should be considered only after all retention options have been proven as ineffective

- Each work out option will have specific qualifications applicable to the homeowner and many will have qualifications applicable to the property.

- Each workout option will present different elements of default protection in the future.

- Each workout plan will present negotiation challenges and options that you must understand.

The following chapters will define the parameters, qualifications, negotiation tools, and transaction confirmation actions for each party. The inclusions of these qualifiers and actions will assist you in developing a negotiation strategy for each homeowner file that you negotiate.

CHAPTER

2

Forbearance

If the homeowner is able to show a personal financial crisis with a definitive end, the lender may consider allowing forbearance.

A forbearance workout allows the homeowner to forego making monthly payments against the note or to make a lower monthly payment than the one stipulated under the note for a period of time. The negotiation as to the amount of monthly payment required during the forbearance period will be based on the type of crisis, homeowner's income, and ability to pay.

The forbearance plan enables the homeowner to negotiate two methods of minimizing the monthly expense of the mortgage during a temporary financial crisis or during the execution of other, simultaneous, loss mitigation options.

The negotiations will enable the homeowner to take a temporary hiatus from the mortgage payment or make a lowered payment for the specified duration of the financial hardship.

The forbearance term may delay the requirement of regular monthly payments during the term the homeowner needs to recover from the temporary financial set back. The purpose of this option is to provide the extra time necessary to enable the homeowner to recapture the financial stability that existed before the default.

The forbearance term may provide the homeowner with a relief from payments while another loss mitigation options, such as the short sale, is completed. The purpose of this option is to enable the homeowner to assist the lender in completing the actions that will prevent a foreclosure.

The temporary forbearance option provides the lender with the opportunity to resume receiving the full principal and interest payment from the homeowner at a specified time without the time investment and expense of a foreclosure and re-sale process. The homeowner retains the ability to stay in their home until the crisis period is over.

A forbearance option applied during the completion of another loss mitigation effort provides the homeowner with the relief from payments necessary to carry out the secondary loss mitigation process.

The options negotiated during the loss mitigation process will depend on the

- resources of the homeowner

- term and type of hardship

- ultimate disposition of the property

The negotiation of the forbearance option should be customized to the needs, ability to pay, and recovery term of the homeowner.

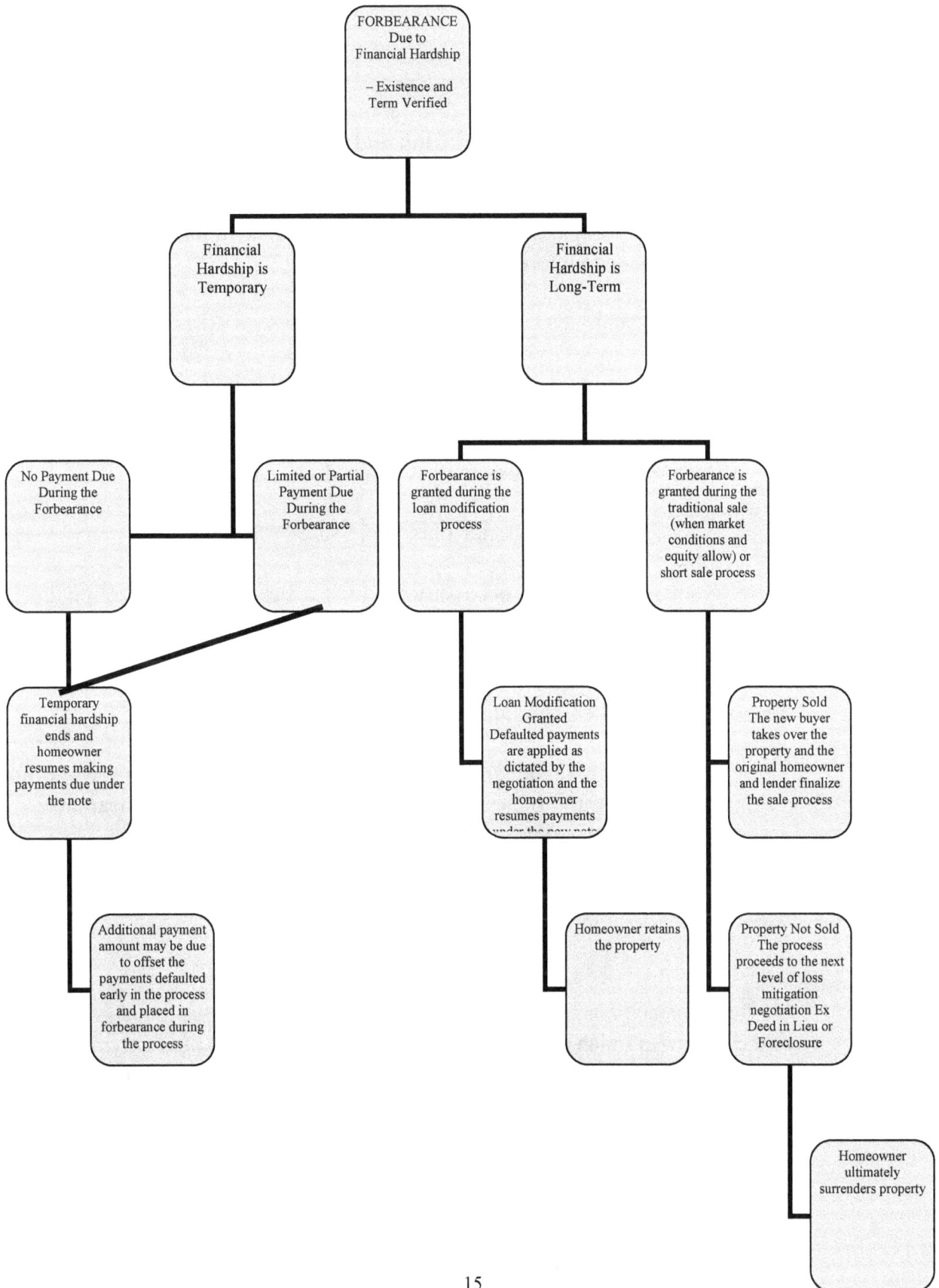

Kenney

FORBEARANCE
Due to
Financial Hardship

– Existence and
Term Verified

Financial
Hardship is
Temporary

Financial
Hardship is
Long-Term

No Payment Due
During the
Forbearance

Limited or Partial
Payment Due
During the
Forbearance

Forbearance is
granted during the
loan modification
process

Forbearance is
granted during the
traditional sale
(when market
conditions and
equity allow) or
short sale process

Temporary
financial hardship
ends and
homeowner
resumes making
payments due under
the note

Loan Modification
Granted
Defaulted payments
are applied as
dictated by the
negotiation and the
homeowner
resumes payments
under the new note

Property Sold
The new buyer
takes over the
property and the
original homeowner
and lender finalize
the sale process

Additional payment
amount may be due
to offset the
payments defaulted
early in the process
and placed in
forbearance during
the process

Homeowner retains
the property

Property Not Sold
The process
proceeds to the next
level of loss
mitigation
negotiation Ex
Deed in Lieu or
Foreclosure

Homeowner
ultimately
surrenders property

The forbearance period will be negotiated for a set term or specified time. These terms will be customized to the situation of the homeowner, planned disposition of the property, and needs of the lender. The negotiations will detail the method of repayment for the arrearages created during the pre-forbearance default and during the agreed upon forbearance.

Term   The terms of the forbearance will be based on the type of hardship the homeowner has encountered.

Hardships are usually either temporary or long-term.

A long-term hardship may require additional loss mitigation actions to assist in curing the default.

Example: Forbearance plus Loan Modification

Forbearance plus Short Sale

The type of workout necessary to cure the default will determine the length of the forbearance offered.

A temporary hardship may be cured by the forbearance without the need for the execution of other, simultaneous work out plans.

If the hardship is temporary, the forbearance may be the only work out option necessary to cure the default and the term of the forbearance will be negotiated based on the term of the hardship.

The forbearance term will be negotiated to correlate to the type of secondary workout necessary for the homeowner.

Repayment Options   If a forbearance plan appears to be an option, the next step is the negotiation of the repayment plan that will apply. The calculations of the repayment are included in the next example. There are three potential repayment options that may apply to the forbearance negotiations.

Forgiveness　　The lender may forgive all or a portion of the payments that would have applied without the forbearance

This forbearance option is rare. Most lenders will require that the homeowner make a good faith effort to repay the amount of the payments that were missed during the forbearance. In special circumstances, the lender may opt to forgive these payments but the financial hardship proof will be heavier

**Resumption +
Catch Up**　　Many lenders will negotiate a plan where the homeowner receives a full or partial forbearance for the negotiated term and then resumes making the payments dictated by the note.

In addition to the monthly payments dictated by the note, the homeowner will make additional payments that are allocated to the arrearages created through the forbearance. The negotiation of the catch up plan should be customized to the situation and means of each homeowner.

An example of a common baseline negotiation point for the lenders is that the repayment plan stipulate that the homeowner resume payments after the forbearance at a rate of 1 ½ times the note stipulated payment. This resumption method could create a hardship for many homeowners.

It is more effective to negotiate a fair and feasible repayment plan that reduces the risk of a future default recurrence.

**Refinance or
Capitalization**　　If the homeowner illustrates that they will have the ability to resume the monthly payments stipulated by the note upon the termination of the temporary hardship but are unable to increase the payment amount by any percentage without creating a new financial hardship a

capitalization of the forbearance payments may be applied. This method of arrearage repayment may also be employed during a loan modification negotiation.

This capitalization enables the payments that were placed in forbearance to be tacked to the end of the loan term.

This allows the homeowner to attain the temporary reduction or removal of the mortgage payments that assist in a regaining financial stability.

Upon the expiration of the forbearance term, the homeowner will resume the stipulated payments without any additional sums due for allocation to the amounts of arrearages that accumulated during the forbearance period.

In this scenario, the only alteration that will be apparent after the expiration of the forbearance is a lengthening of the loan term. This lengthening tacks all of the payments to the back end of the loan.

The homeowner will typically be required to sign a new note or complete a refinance package for this negotiation to apply.

Repayment Calculations

When the loss mitigation workout enables the homeowner to retain possession of the property, the forbearance agreement will define the method of repayment for the payments that were in defaulted before the creation of the agreement and then postponed during the forbearance term.

Day 1-90 (3 months)	Day 90-210 (3-7 months)	Day 210 – end of mortgage term (7 months – 30 years or term)	Day 210-630 (7 – 28 months post forbearance)	Day 660 (21 months)
Homeowner falls behind on mortgage payments. Forbearance of 120 days approved by lender	Homeowner suspends all payments for 120 days during recovery from financial crises	Homeowner resumes making stipulated monthly payment (regular)	Homeowner adds ½ of total payment to regular stipulated payment to 'catch up' the arrearages resulting from the forbearance	Accumulated arrearage repaid, homeowner makes payments stipulated

Figure 2:1 – Forbearance Timeline

Example: Homeowner falls 90 days (3 months) behind on a mortgage that dictates monthly payments of $550.00

Homeowner contacts loss mitigation department and a 120-day (4 months) full forbearance workout is approved

Homeowner delays making any payments over the subsequent 120-day period

The temporary financial hardship ends on day 210 (7-months from the initial defaulted payment)

Homeowner resumes making the stipulated note payments on day 210 (7-months) of $550.00 per month until the loan term is paid in full or the property is refinanced.

Homeowner makes an additional payment of ½ the regular mortgage payment due $275.00 to offset the amount of the payments accumulated during the forbearance term.

These payments would need to total the costs of the default and forbearance payments

7 months	x	$550.00	=	$3850.00
$550	/	½	=	$ 275.00

$3850 .00   / $275.00   =   14 months

The homeowner makes an additional $275.00 payment each month for 14 months

This example does not take into account any late payment penalty, interest accumulations or other costs negotiated during the transaction.

Full or Partial

A forbearance of payments may be granted for the entire amount of the payment due under the note. The forbearance may also be granted for only a portion of the normal payment due under the note.

Example: Homeowner falls 90 days (3 months) behind on a mortgage that dictates monthly payments of $550.00

Homeowner contacts loss mitigation department and a 120-day (4 months) PARTIAL forbearance is approved

Homeowner delays ½ of each payment due during the 120 day period and makes the remaining payment on the regular due date

The temporary financial hardship ends on day 210 (7 months from the initial defaulted payment)

Homeowner resumes making the stipulated note payments on day 210 (7 months) of $550.00 per month until the loan term is paid in full or the property is refinanced.

Homeowner makes an additional payment of ½ the regular mortgage payment due $275.00 to offset the amount of the payments accumulated during the forbearance term.

These payments would need to total the costs of the default and forbearance payments. Remember in this example the first 3 payments were in arrears at the time of the forbearance and the next 4 payments were paid at a rate of 50% of the amount due.

	3 months	x	$550.00 =		$1650.00
+	4 months	x	$275.00 =		$1100.00
			=		$2750.00
	$2750 .00	/	$275.00 =		10 months

The homeowner makes an additional $275.00 payment each month for 10 months

This example does not take into account any late payment penalty, interest accumulations or other costs negotiated during the transaction.

Qualification

During the assessment portion of the loss mitigation process, the loss mitigation specialist will gather certain information, documentation, and details from the homeowner. Each loss mitigation option requires that the homeowner

- Meet the qualifications set forth by the lender

- Verify the need for loss mitigation negotiations

- Verify that the application of the loss mitigation options will enable the homeowner to regain the capacity to resume payments if that is a component of the negotiations

The loss mitigation specialist will be responsible for qualifying the homeowner, obtaining verifications, and planning the negotiation package for remittal to the lender or loss mitigation supervisor.

Verification   Before negotiating a forbearance plan with the homeowner, you should obtain verification of the existence and cause of the hardship.

Example: Temporary job interruption

Proof of unemployment claim

Proof of injury

Other proof as dictated by the hardship

The verifications that are necessary to prove the homeowner's hardship will vary depending on the situation. Any verification must be provided from an independent third party. The verification should illustrate the facts set forth by the homeowner. Additional details related to verifications are included later in the course.

Financial Need   To qualify for the forbearance options the homeowner must illustrate that certain minimum financial hardships exist. The forbearance is, by nature a temporary corrective action.

Financial Hardship   The homeowner must illustrate that the financial crisis that relates to the delinquency is sudden and temporary.

Example: Verifiable temporary loss of income

Verifiable temporary increase in living expenses

Future Stability   The ability to

- correct the delinquency through gradual repayment of the arrearages

- maintain the payments stipulated under the note after the forbearance term expires

- minimize the likelihood of the event recurrence in the future through the illustration that the current financial crisis is a single-occurrence

The forbearance requirements relating to a proven future stability on the part of the homeowner may be excepted if the homeowner is negotiating forbearance in combination with another loss mitigation alternative such as a refinance or property sale option.

Occupancy

Most lenders require that the property be an owner occupied primary residence.

> Second residences, vacation homes, and investment property typically do not qualify for forbearance options.

Many lenders will have screened the intended occupancy of the property at the time that that the original mortgage loan was granted. The lender may review the statements of the homeowner on the original mortgage application and review the occupancy declaration that was completed during the closing of the original mortgage loan. It is important that the loss mitigation specialist ask the homeowner about the contents of these documents during the analysis portion of the loss mitigation process. If any questionable entries may exist on these documents, the inclusions will need to be addressed before most lenders will approve a loss mitigation package.

The homeowner may be required to complete a new occupancy declaration as part of the negotiation process. This occupancy declaration will state the homeowner's intention to use the property as a primary residence during and after the application of the loss mitigation options.

Property Value

Forbearance negotiations will typically not require an inspection or an appraisal of the property as value is not an issue in homeowner retention forbearance negotiations.

If the forbearance request is to be combined with other loss mitigation plans such as a loan modification, property value and condition may become an element in the negotiation process.

If the surrender of the property through a short sale or the modification of a loan is an element to the negotiations, the lender will typically request an appraisal or market comparison study on the property.

Property Condition

At times, the lender may require proof of the condition and value of the subject property before considering a forbearance offer.

The negotiations will define the minimum condition requirements of the property.

> The theory behind the property condition requirements are that many homeowners will be unable or unwilling to resume regular payments on a property whose condition is greatly deteriorated or whose value is exponentially lower than the mortgage principal balance.

Some lenders will consider granting an extension of the forbearance to accommodate the costs of necessary property condition maintenance and repairs.

> The possibility of a forbearance extension specifically allocated toward enabling the property owner to complete the necessary repairs will often result in enhanced inspection requirements and homeowner certifications.

This options is most often applied for property that will ultimately be offered for sale rather than retained by the homeowner but is a viable negotiation point in any transaction.

Title Search

The lender may require a title search on the property to determine the status of any other liens against the property that may place the ability of the homeowner and security of the loan at risk. This requirement is often used in property surrender negotiations, but may apply to a forbearance if the credit report illustrates that the homeowner has multiple other bills that may place the future stability of payment against the note at a higher risk for default

The mortgage holder will order a title search as a part of the negotiation stage of the forbearance workout. If the title search uncovers junior liens or other encumbrances, the forbearance plan may proceed as planned if the surplus income of the homeowner illustrates that the cost of these liens will be manageable after the hardship term expires. If the homeowner cannot illustrate an ability to make payments on these liens and the mortgage note, other loss mitigation options may need to be considered.

Agreement   A written agreement detailing all of the negotiated points must be executed between the lender and the homeowner. This agreement will define the

- Term of forbearance

- Percentage of the payment placed in forbearance

- Percentage of the payment the homeowner must pay during the forbearance period

- Frequency of any required payments during forbearance

- Special term of forbearance applicable to property repairs or maintenance costs

- Method of recovery of the payments under the forbearance agreement

    Gradual repayment

    Forgiveness

    Capitalization

- An acknowledgement of the missed mortgage payments (previous delinquency) and handling of these payments

- A notice that a failure on the part of the homeowner to comply with the negotiated terms of the forbearance plan my result in the lender initiating a foreclosure process will often be included by the lender representative or loss mitigation specialist

Combination   The forbearance option may be negotiated as a stand-alone solution or be negotiated as an element in other loss mitigation workout.

    Example: Forbearance until a short sale is achieved

            Forbearance during loan modification negotiations

Forbearance during the short refinance process.

NOTE: HUD Insured Loans may have special requirements relating to the criteria, minimum values, negotiation percentages, processes, costs, and other matters. If you are negotiating a special forbearance transaction that involves a HUD Insured Loan, please see the applicable before proceeding with the negotiation processes.

Common Negotiation Elements

- Provide the homeowner with a temporary relief from all of a portion of the required payments to enable a financial recover

- Fully reinstate the loan, except if combined with mortgage modification

- A determination of the method for the allocation of late fees and penalties – often the mortgage lender will agree to refrain from assessing any fees while the homeowner is performing under the terms of a special forbearance plan.

- The allocation of reasonable foreclosure costs and late fees accrued prior to the execution of the special forbearance agreement - some lenders will require that the homeowner include costs incurred prior to the loss mitigation workout. The repayment of these costs is an element of the negotiation process and common options are to combine them as part of the repayment schedule, wrap them into a loan modification or refinance option negotiated in cooperation with the forbearance, or forgive them under special circumstances.

- Forbearance term customized to meet the ability to the homeowner to resume the normal payment process

SPECIAL FORBEARANCE INTERVIEW AND FILE CHECKLIST

Homeowner: _____

Requirement	Verification (Date, Amount, Source of Information etc.)
1. Has the homeowner experienced a verifiable loss of income or increase in living expenses?	
2. Is the term of this loss of income or increased living expense temporary?	
3. Length of expected hardship?	
4. Is the property owner occupied?	
5. Is the owner occupied status verifiable by the original mortgage application or closing occupancy declaration?	
6. Did the homeowner receive the How to Avoid Foreclosure brochure or obtain the services of a loss mitigation specialist?	
7. Will the loan be more than 90 and less than 365 days delinquent on the effective date of the agreement? (show number of days)	
8. Did the income analysis to determine the homeowner's current inability to pay the debt include:	
• A financial statement provided by the homeowner	
• A credit report	
• Income/Expense Verifications	

• Evidence the homeowner hardship is temporary	
9. Did the income analysis to determine the homeowner's ability to repay the debt after the forbearance include:	
• A financial statement provided by the homeowner	
• A credit report	
• Income/Expense Verifications	
• Evidence the homeowner can support the payment schedule	
10. The homeowner's current DTI ratio	
11. The homeowner's expected DTI ratio	
12. When and why will the homeowner's income increase?	
13. Has an inspection determined that the property has no adverse conditions affecting continued occupancy?	
14. Does the title search indicate that junior liens exist against the property?	
15. Does the homeowner's expected income support the ability to resume payments with these junior liens in place?	
16. Does the written agreement executed by the homeowner:	
• Clearly define the terms and frequency of repayment	

• Offer relief not available through a normal repayment plan	
• State that failure to comply may result in foreclosure	
• Limit the total default to 12 months or less	
17. If the special forbearance agreement culminates in a modification or short sale, has the proposed type and date of the action been negotiated?	

Figure 2:2 Forbearance Sample Form – File Checklist
This form is included for reference purposes only. You should obtain the applicable HUD or Lender forms for use in a negotiation.

Package Inclusion Checklist

Hardship Verification Forms

- Existence

- Term

Used to determine the need and applicability of the forbearance

Used to negotiation the term of the forbearance

Occupancy Status Verification

- At original mortgage application

- At original mortgage closing

- Present

Used to verify the ability to negotiate a forbearance agreement under lender guidelines

DTI Assessment

- Present

  Used to prove the need for forbearance

  Used to negotiate the percentage of payment placed in forbearance

  Used to negotiate the amount and frequency of payments during forbearance

- Expiration of Hardship (with repayment)

  Used to negotiate the term of the forbearance

  Used to negotiate the method of repayment for the arrearages

- Expiration of Hardship (post repayment)

  Used to prove the stability of the homeowner post-loss mitigation intervention

Surplus Income Assessment

- Present

  Used to negotiated the amount and frequency of payments during forbearance

- Expiration of Hardship

  Used to negotiate the repayment of arrearages post forbearance

Credit Report

Used to confirm existence / amount of subordinate liens

Used to establish DTI Ratio

Title Search

Used to confirm existence / amount of subordinate liens

Property Inspection / Appraisal

Used to establish value and condition of the property

Used to negotiate special property improvement element

You will complete a pre-qualification assessment with each homeowner before beginning the process of planning a loss mitigation strategy. A pre-qualification assessment questionnaire is included in a later chapter. You should practice completing the assessment questionnaire to ensure that you include all applicable elements in each homeowner interview. The elements of the checklist included are the most essential in a forbearance negotiation, and will be the components you include within each package you submit to the lender for consideration.

CHAPTER

3

Loan Modification

Loan modification is a process where the lender and homeowner agree on new mortgage terms that are acceptable to both parties.

The homeowner must negotiate the new terms so that they are able to manage future mortgage payments.

The lender will strive to negotiate new mortgage terms that provide them with the highest level of investment return and security.

Common loan modification changes include

- Lowering the interest rate

- Increasing the loan term

- Lowering the principal balance of the loan

- Forgiving penalties, past due interest or other surplus charges

- Capitalization of delinquent principal, interest and other charges

- Re-amortization of the new principal balance over a new loan term

The loan modification will be a permanent change to the loan of the homeowner.

The benefits of the modification are that the lender retains some ability to recapture the value of the loan from the original homeowner without incurring the expense of a foreclosure or re-sale process on the property. The foreclosure or short sale process is often

- time-consuming

- expensive

- results in the lender reducing the sales price of the property to a figure that is lower than the principal amount owed on of the original note

Modification is typically used to reduce a homeowner's required monthly payment to a level in keeping with their ability to pay. This loss mitigation tools should be considered whenever the cause of the financial crises is expected to be of a longer duration.

Loan modifications can be negotiated for any homeowner who can illustrate that the current loan terms present a financial hardship due to a verifiable change in circumstances.

Example: Rate Adjustment

Income reduction of a longer-term duration

The homeowner must be able to illustrate that the modification will enable them to maintain the newly defined payments.

Loan Characteristics

Certain loans contain characteristics that make them a higher candidate for modification that other mortgage loans. These loans are those that

- Have a higher than market average interest rate

- Have lower LTV ratios

- Have an equity position that enables the capitalization of costs associated with the default or modification process

- Have a shorter-term repayment plan

Lenders will typically negotiate a modification that enables the homeowner to obtain a fully amortized, fixed rate loan. Any lender who is operating in cooperation with the governmentally mandated guidelines must provide a fully amortized, fixed rate loan when accepting the loan modification option as a result of the loss mitigation negotiation.

Example: Loans that have a longer payment history or that were originally amortized over a shorter term may be re-amortized to extend the loan term thus lowering the monthly payment

UNDERSTANDING THE BENEFITS OF
LOAN MODIFICATION

Modifications made to the homeowner's mortgage can provide the relief necessary to stabilize the homeowner's financial situation, cure the current default situation, and maximize the likelihood than the homeowner will maintain all future payments under the note. The loan modification does present a loss potential for the lender, but often, these losses are lower than the losses that would apply if the lender were to foreclose on the property and attempt to sell it to a new buyer in the current real estate market. The effect of loss mitigation on the homeowner currently in default is beneficial. The homeowner will be able to retain the property, assume new liabilities more in keeping with the homeowner's ability to pay, and possibly match the loan principal amount to the present market value of the property. All of these elements increase the financial stability of the homeowner.

Interest Rate Calculations

Loan Modification often includes a revision of the interest rate that applies to the loan. An interest rate alteration can have an extreme effect on the monthly payment due from the homeowner.

Example

Loan Amount	Interest Rate 6.250 30 year amortization	Interest Rate 10.375 30 year amortization	Payment Difference
$100,000	$ 615.72	$ 905.41	$289.69
$125,000	$ 769.65	$1131.76	$362.11
$150,000	$ 923.58	$1358.11	$434.53
$175,000	$1077.51	$1584.76	$507.25
$200,000	$1231.43	$1810.81	$579.38
$225,000	$1385.36	$2037.17	$651.81

Figure 3:1 Example – Interest Rate affect on monthly P&I Payment

The table illustrates the immediate effect that a modification of the loan interest rate may have on the ability of the homeowner to make the monthly payment on the mortgage note.

Many of the loan modification negotiations you will complete will relate to loans that were issued under a classification known as 'sub-prime'. The interest rate of sub-prime loans will often be much higher than the rate applied to many other types of loans. The variation in rates caused when the loan type is an adjustable rate that has now begun to adjust will be much greater.

Many lenders will have internal interest rate sheets that will be used to help make a determination of the rate that may be negotiated as part of the loan modification process.

In order to consider loan modification options, you will need to determine the interest rate or price that may apply to the transaction.

The offered interest rate is a point of negotiation. You should calculate the payment based on various interest rate ranges and term units. This will enable you to open negotiations that meet the lender criteria

    Example: Debt-To-Income Ratio

    Maximum rate reduction limits

The pricing of each loss mitigation negotiation will be subject to the offer by the lender. You should gain an understanding of how the lender will price the potential loan modification and the way that this new price or interest rate will affect the homeowner's ability to resume normal payments.

- Before beginning the pricing of the loan, you should review the rate sheet to determine if there are any restrictions to pricing.

  Restrictions will include any internal requirements and applicable laws regarding loan pricing.

  Example: Loans under $50,000 may not be eligible for loan modification.

- If the rate sheet includes qualifying information, it should match the data detailed within the assessment of the loan guideline matrix detailed within the refinance chapter.

  Not all rate sheets will include qualifying information.

- You should familiarize yourself with the format of the rate sheet.

  Every lender has a variation on the rate sheet format that they use. The rate sheets will contain the same basic information. The layout used will be different.

- Locate the preferred loan terms for your homeowner.

  Example: 30 year fixed

  Example: 40 year fixed

- Locate the LTV your homeowner requires.

- Locate the pricing you must obtain.

  Example: PAR

- Locate the corresponding interest rate.

  This rate will be applied to determine the new payment that may apply to the modified loan.

The homeowner must be able to have a provable ability to meet this payment obligation after the modification.

The baseline rate determined through the assessment of the lender's modification rate sheet will be a negotiation point in the loss mitigation negotiations that lead to a loan modification for your homeowner.

SAMPLE RATE SHEET

Grade	LTV	40 Year Fixed		30 Year Fixed	
		Par	<1.00>	Par	<1.00>
A 660+	97%	6.500	7.000	7.000	7.500
Mortgage 0X30	95%	6.125	6.625	6.500	7.000
Consumer 1X30	90%	6.000	6.500	6.125	6.625
BK/For 3/ 3	85%	5.875	6.125	6.000	6.500
DTI 41%	80%	5.750	6.250	5.875	6.375
	75%	5.625	6.125	5.750	6.250
B	95%	7.125	7.500	8.000	8.500
620-669	90%	7.000	7.375	7.875	8.375
Mtg 1x30	85%	6.625	7.000	7.500	8.000
Con any	80%	6.500	6.875	7.125	7.625
BK / For 3/ 3	75%	6.125	6.500	6.875	7.375
DTI 45%	70%	5.875	6.125	6.500	7.000
C	90%	7.500	8.000	8.500	
590-619	85%	7.375	7.875	8.375	
Mtg 2X60	80%	7.000	7.500	8.000	
Con any	75%	6.875	7.125	7.875	8.125
BK / For 2/ 2	70%	6.500	6.875	7.500	7.875

DTI 47%						
D		85%	7.875	8.375		
560-589		80%	7.500	8.000	8.500	
Mtg	90+	75%	7.125	7.625	8.375	
Con	any	70%	6.875	7.125	8.250	
BK/ For	2/ 2					
DTI 50%						

Figure 3:2 Sample Rate Sheet
This form is included for reference purposes only. You should obtain the applicable HUD or Lender forms for use in a negotiation.

Pre-pricing Quick List

- Qualifying level of your homeowner

- LTV required by your homeowner

- CLTV required by your homeowner

- Amortization Term desired by your homeowner

To determine your homeowner's approval level, you will want to refer to the credit scoring forms you completed earlier.

You will also need to verify the DTI Ratios to be certain they fall within the guidelines of the level you wish to place your homeowners.

- Note that each level has different LTV options.

  In general, the lower the LTV as compared to the maximum allowed the lower the interest rate.

- The higher the credit-grade status of your homeowners the better interest rate they can expect.

- Keep in mind that using the maximum available options for your Credit Grade typically will increase the interest rate.

PRICING THE LOANRate Sheet Quick Guide

Credit Grade	You will need to refer to your credit worksheet to determine the credit grade for which your homeowner's will qualify. Upon reviewing your Product Matrix and Guidelines, you should have developed you own system for charting the credit grade of your homeowner's package under the various programs you are considering.	Each program will have a different set of terminology for their credit grades. Many will put the basic minim requirements for each grade level on the rate sheet so you can double-check the credit history as you price the potential modification.
Credit Score	You will want to verify that the credit score you have determined as applicable for the program meets the minimum requirements for the grade level that you are pricing.	Keep in mind that different lender's use a different score. Some use the middle credit score ranked by numbers and some will use the most regionally accurate score for the homeowner's location.
Mortgage History	Each credit grade on the rate sheet included lists the number and the time allowed for that grade with regard to mortgage late payments in the last 12 months.	If the mortgage history is not on the credit report, you will need to provide documentation proving the mortgage or rental history status over the prior 12-month period.
BK/FC	Credit grades often require that a bankruptcy or foreclosure be 'seasoned" for a period. This refers to the date of discharge.	If the date is not apparent on the credit report, you will need to provide documentation proving the discharge date.
Consumer Credit	As with mortgage history most Credit Grades will require that, the consumer history meets certain minimums.	Some Credit Grade sheets will remove consumer history as a criterion. These lenders rely on credit scores to reflect the consumer history.

Debt Ratio	Many rate sheets provide you with the maximum debt ratio allowed under that grade. If your homeowner's exceed this ratio, they will be dropped to the nearest grade whose minimum requirements they do meet.	Bear in mind that the Debt Ratios must be calculated twice to illustrate a need for the loan modification on the part of your homeowner. The DTI you will use during the potential pricing assessment is the one that is created THROUGH the modification or the post-modification DTI Ratio.
LTV (Loan To Value)	This section lists the maximum loan to value options available for each credit grade	You will note that there are listings below the maximum LTV available. In most cases, the lower the actual LTV as compared to the maximum LTV allowed the lower the interest rate offered.
Amortization Term	The next columns show the program term options	
PAR	Directly below the term option you will see PAR, <1.00> To price at par means that there are not points included in the interest rate	To price at <1.00> means that the lender is incorporating costs of the loan into the interest rate. This could be commission for the loan officer in a traditional refinance, costs assessed by the lender in another form of refinance. This is known as wrapping points or being paid on the back-end.
Pricing	You will now incorporate all of the options to arrive at an interest rate quote. First, find the correct credit grade, determine your required loan to value, and then follow the column over to the correct loan term option and pricing (back end points).	The rate shown is the interest rate you will use as a basis for the feasibility of a loan modification plan to assist your homeowners out of the financial crises.

Figure 3:3 Sample Rate Sheet Key
This form is included for reference purposes only. You should obtain the applicable HUD or Lender forms for use in a negotiation

We have included some sample credit reports in the Chapter Career Building Tools. We recommend you use the samples and forms included to practice preliminary product assessments and rate quotes.

The interest rate will be based upon a financial index. These indexes set a base rate and the lender then places add ons, often termed basis points in the lending arena, to calculate the interest rate that will apply to a transaction.

The applicable rate sheet may change on a daily basis or even more frequently depending on the lender with whom you are working. It is essential that you negotiate the best interest rate terms and thus the best monthly payment that you can for the transaction. The purpose of the loan modification is to ensure that the homeowner will be able to maintain the newly defined payments on the mortgage. If you do not ensure that the new payment agreement meets the payment capability illustrated by the DTI Ratio Calculations you complete with the homeowner, the risk of another default remains high even after the loan modification.

Amortization Changes

Loan Modification may also encompass a change to the amortization term of the note. The previous illustration shows the manner that payments will change as a result of the application of different interest rates. The previous chart illustrated these changes based on a 30-year amortization term.

The application of different amortization terms will also affect the monthly payment requirements of the note.

The following chart defines the payment changes that will result if the interest rate on a loan remains the same but the amortization term is changed.

Loan Amount	15 year amortization Interest Rate 6.250	30 year amortization Interest Rate 6.250	Payment Difference
$100,000	$ 857.42	$ 615.72	$241.70
$125,000	$1071.78	$ 769.65	$302.13
$150,000	$1286.13	$ 923.58	$362.55

$175,000	$1500.49	$1077.51	$422.98
$200,000	$1714.85	$1231.43	$483.42
$225,000	$1929.20	$1385.36	$543.84

Figure 3:4 Sample affect of amortization changes
This form is included for reference purposes only. You should obtain the applicable HUD or Lender forms for use in a negotiation

The extension of the amortization term may have a dramatic impact on the monthly payment required under the loan terms. 15-year, 25-year, and 30-year terms have long been common within the mortgage lending industry. Some lenders are now offering even longer amortization terms to enable the homeowner to spread the repayment over an even longer term.

Even a homeowner who is currently making payments on the maximum term amortization schedule may benefit from a loan term alteration if they have been making payments on the note for a period of time sufficient to build equity into their transaction.

Example:	Homeowner Original Note	$200,000.00
	30-year amortization payment	$ 1,231.43
	Principal Balance at Default	$187,000.00
	Payment at re-amortization	$ 1,151.39

Under this scenario, you do not change the term of the amortization.

You take the new principal balance owed on the note as a result of the homeowner making payments on their mortgage over the years preceding the default and amortize that as a new loan basis amount.

The payment alteration in this scenario will be dependent on the equity position built up by the homeowner through regular payments.

The changes to the monthly payment achieved through this method may not be as dramatic as those generated through other modification methods. You will find that even an 80.00 per month change to the required monthly payment can have a great enough effect to cure the default of some homeowners. Other homeowners will require more intensive modification negotiation to ensure that they are financially capable of maintaining the new mortgage payments.

BLENDED OR COMBINATION MODIFICATION

Using a combination of interest rate reduction and amortization term changes can lower the payment a sufficient amount to stabilize many of the homeowners with whom you will work.

Example – Blended Modification

Loan Amount	Current Initial Interest Rate 10.375 15 year amortization	Rate Change ONLY Interest Rate Reduction to 6.250 15 year amortization	Rate PLUS Amortization Interest Rate 6.250 Amortization Change to 30-Year Amortization	Total Blended Modification Change
$100,000	$1097.66	$ 857.42	$ 615.72	$ 481.94
$125,000	$1372.08	$1071.78	$ 769.65	$ 602.43
$150,000	$1646.49	$1286.13	$ 923.58	$ 722.91
$175,000	$1920.91	$1500.49	$1077.51	$ 843.40
$200,000	$2195.32	$1714.85	$1231.43	$ 963.89
$225,000	$2469.74	$1929.20	$1385.36	$1084.38

Figure 3:5 Sample effect of blended modification
This form is included for reference purposes only. You should obtain the applicable HUD or Lender forms for use in a negotiation.

Loan modification negotiation can include all or only some of the potential note changes. It is critical that you complete a comprehensive assessment of the homeowners current and expected DTI position.

This assessment will enable you to determine if loan modification negotiations will benefit the homeowner enough to stabilize the payment capability and decrease the risk of a potential default in the future. You will also custom fit the negotiations to suit the homeowner. Most lenders will decline a modification package that includes more modifications than are necessary to stabilize the financial status of the homeowner.

Qualification

To qualify for a modification, most lenders will require that the homeowner meet certain minimum qualifications.

During the assessment portion of the loss mitigation process, the loss mitigation specialist will gather certain information, documentation, and details from the homeowner. Each loss mitigation option requires that the homeowner

- Meet the qualifications set forth by the lender

- Verify the need for loss mitigation negotiations

- Verify that the application of the loss mitigation options will enable the homeowner to regain the capacity to resume payments if that is a component of the negotiations

The loss mitigation specialist will be responsible for qualifying the homeowner, obtaining verifications, and planning the negotiation package for remittal to the lender or loss mitigation supervisor.

Verification   Before negotiating a loan modification plan with the homeowner, you should obtain verification of the existence and cause of the hardship.

Example: Interest Rate Adjustment

Proof of original note and new interest rate PLUS proof of inability to meet new rate dictated obligations

Long-Term Income Decrease

Proof of new income

Proof of adjustment to disability income

Proof of the death of one spouse

Other proof as dictated by the hardship

The verifications that are necessary to prove the homeowner's hardship will vary depending on the situation. Any verification must be provided from an independent third party. The verification should illustrate the facts set forth by the homeowner. Additional details related to verifications are included later in the course.

Financial Need   To qualify for a loan modification, the homeowner must be able to illustrate that a change in circumstances exists that has created the default situation.

Mitigation Aide   The homeowner must be able to illustrate that income is sufficient to maintain the new loan payment that will be defined by the loan modification terms.

- If the income is sufficient to meet the current loan payment requirements, the lender will typically decline the modification request

- If the homeowner is suffering a temporary income reduction, many lenders will decline the modification request and present a counter negotiation under another option such as the forbearance

- If the homeowner is suffering a long-term income reduction that cannot be cured through lesser mitigation efforts and makes the payment of the current mortgage note impossible, the homeowner must be able to illustrate that they will be able to meet the obligations after the modified terms have been applied to the note.

Occupancy   Most lenders require that any negotiation for loan modification be for an owner occupied primary residence.

If the property is a second home, vacation home, investment property, or other type of non-owner occupied property most lenders will decline a loan modification request.

Many lenders will have screened the intended occupancy of the property at the time that that the original mortgage loan was granted.

The lender may review the statements of the homeowner on the original mortgage application and review the occupancy declaration that was completed during the closing of the original mortgage loan.

It is important that the loss mitigation specialist ask the homeowner about the contents of these documents during the analysis portion of the loss mitigation process. If any questionable entries may exist on these documents, the inclusions will need to be addressed before most lenders will approve a loss mitigation package.

The homeowner may be required to complete a new occupancy declaration as part of the negotiation process. This occupancy declaration will state the homeowner's intention to use the property as a primary residence during and after the application of the loss mitigation options.

Property Value Loan modifications will typically not require an inspection or an appraisal of the property if the proposed modifications are limited to alterations to the rate, term, or amortization methods. If the loan modification negotiations include a request to lower the principal balance on the note, the lender will require proof that the market value of the property is less than the amount owed.

An appraisal or market comparison study on the property will provide proof of the current market value of the property. The market value indicated of the property must typically be lower than the amount owed on the note for the lender to consider a principal reduction as a modification option.

A segment relating to understanding appraisal inclusions and value methods is included later in the course. It is important that you understand the elements that are considered with regard to the value of a property and also the effect that the ratings applied by the appraiser may have on the negotiation processes.

Property Condition

If an appraisal is completed on the property as part of the negotiation or if lender required inspections are required, the property must usually meet condition criteria in order for the lender to approve the modification agreement.

If the property condition shows deterioration or the need for extensive repairs, the lender may require that the homeowner complete these repairs as part of the modification agreement.

> The theory behind the property condition requirements is that many homeowners may opt against complying with the newly modified terms if the property condition continues to deteriorate.

> Another consideration is that the expense of maintaining a deteriorating or damaged residence may create another financial crisis in the future resulting in a second default scenario.

If the property requires repairs and the homeowner is unable to pay for the completion of these repairs, other loss mitigation options may need to be considered.

The lender will rarely capitalize the costs of these repairs into the newly structured loan. If the equity position of the homeowner is strong enough to support the payment of the principal amount of the loan, any subordinate liens, and the cost of repairs, most lenders will decline the principal reduction modification request and counter offer a delinquent refinance or forbearance to facilitate a sale of the property.

Title Search

The lender may require that a title search on the property be completed. This helps to determine the status of ay other liens against the property that may need to be discharged prior to the modification agreement or that place the security of the lender at risk.

The lender will typically require that all subordinate liens against the property be discharged or released before a principal reduction loan modification can be finalized. If the loan modification relates only to changes in rates and terms, the homeowner must be able to prove that they have the ability to meet all lien obligations after the modification in order for the lender to ensure adequate security against future default.

The mortgage holder will order a title search as a part of the processing stage of the negotiation. If the title search uncovers junior liens or other encumbrances not illustrated elsewhere in the homeowner's profile, the loan modification plan may processed as planned if the homeowner can illustrate that the payment of these debts falls within the DTI Ratio required by the lender. If the homeowner cannot illustrate the ability to make the payments on these liens and the newly modified loan, other loss mitigation options may need to be considered.

Agreement

The written agreement finalizing a loan modification option must dictate the

- newly defined loan terms including

  ➢ interest rate

  ➢ principal financed

  ➢ amortization method

  ➢ amortization term

  ➢ any special conditions

- a detailed statement of all advances that are necessary to reinstate the PITI payment

- detail relating to any legal, administrative and penalty costs that may apply

Combination

The loan modification option may be negotiated as a stand-alone loss mitigation effort or combined with other loss mitigation options.

Example: Loan Modification with a term of Special Forbearance

NOTE: HUD Insured Loans may have special requirements relating to the criteria, minimum values, negotiation percentages, processes, costs, and other matters. If you are negotiating a loss mitigation transaction that involves a HUD Insured Loan, please see the applicable GOVERNMENTAL REQUIREMENTS before proceeding with the negotiation processes.

You must gain the ability to pre-qualify a potential modification before submitting the package to the lender for approval, counter-offer, or decline. The chapter relating to qualifying the homeowner and the property will provide you with enhanced details regarding the methods that a lender will use to determine the potential modifications that may enable the homeowner to achieve financial stability and prevent future default situations. It is essential to your career as a loss mitigation specialist that you gain an understanding of how interest rates are calculated on a file and how different rate and term options will affect the ability of the homeowner to meet the obligations created during a loan modification.

Common Negotiation Elements

- Modifications result in a fully amortized fixed rate loan

- Modification fully reinstates the loan

- Note interest rate reduction to a level equal to other market interest rates.

    NOTE: Note rates may actually be reduced below the market rate if the additional reduction assists in stabilizing the homeowner and prevents a full default.

- All or a portion of the default arrearage or forbearance term accumulation may be capitalized into the mortgage balance.

- Reduction in the principal balance of the loan

    The modified principal balance may exceed 100% loan-to-value and may exceed the principal balance of the original note if certain arrearages are capitalized onto the loan balance.

- Re-amortizing of the total unpaid amount due over the remaining term of the mortgage to a new or higher amortization term

- Forgiveness or capitalization of penalties, past due interest, defaulted payments or other surplus charges

LOAN MODIFICATION CHECKLIST

Homeowner: _____

Requirement	Verification (Date, Amount, Source of Information etc.)
1. Has the homeowner experienced a verifiable loss of income or increase in living expenses?	
2. Is the term of the loss if income or increased living expense temporary or long term?	
3. Is the increased living expense a result of a change in the interest rate of an adjustable rate loan?	
4. Does the homeowner have a commitment to continue to occupy the property as his or her primary residence?	
5. Is the owner occupied status verifiable by the original mortgage application or closing occupancy declaration?	
6. Did the homeowner receive the How to Avoid Foreclosure brochure?	
7. Will the loan be more than 90 days delinquent on the date of execution and funding? (show number of days)?	

8. Did the income analysis to determine the homeowner's current inability ability to repay the debt include:	
• A financial statement provided by the homeowner	
• A credit report	
• Income/expense verifications	
9. What is the pre-modification DTI?	
10. Post-modification DTI?	
11. Why can't the default be cured by a special forbearance arrangement?	
12. Has a property appraisal been completed to determine the current market value of the property?	
13. Current Market Value	
14. Has an inspection determined that the property has no adverse conditions affecting the continued occupancy?	
15. Has a title search established first lien status of the modified loan?	
• Will release of junior liens be required	
• Will title endorsement be required	
16. Does the homeowner's DTI Assessment support the ability to maintain the modified payment with the junior liens in place?	

17. Does the written modification agreement executed by the homeowner:	
• Include all advances necessary to reinstate the principal, interest, taxes and insurance?	
• Exclude all legal and administrative costs?	
• Define the terms of the newly modified note?	
• Offer relief not available through a normal repayment plan?	
• State that failure to comply with the terms of the modified note may result in foreclosure.	

Figure 3:6 Sample Modification Checklist
This form is included for reference purposes only. You should obtain the applicable HUD or Lender forms for use in a negotiation

Assessment Inclusion Checklist

Hardship Verification Forms

- Existence

- Term

- Cause

Used to determine the need and applicability of the loan modification option

Used to negotiation the terms of the modification

Occupancy Status Verification

- At original mortgage application

- At original mortgage closing

- Present

Used to verify the ability to negotiate a loan modification agreement under lender guidelines

DTI Assessment

- Present

    Used to prove the need for loan modification

    Used to negotiate the type of loan modification necessary to cure the default: Interest Rate Change, Principal Balance Reduction, Amortization Term, and Cost Capitalization

Credit Report

Used to confirm existence / amount of subordinate liens

Used to establish DTI Ratio

Title Search

Used to confirm existence / amount of subordinate liens

Property Inspection / Appraisal

Used to establish value and condition of the property

Used to negotiate a principal balance reduction

CHAPTER

4

Refinance

A refinance of the current mortgage is a desirable option for many homeowners if they meet the qualifications necessary to secure a new loan.

A refinance may be qualified as a traditional refinance or a short refinance.

A homeowner who contacts a loss mitigation specialist before a default situation exists may be a candidate for a refinance transaction rather than a loss mitigation process. The guidelines and qualification parameters of the lender must be met in order for a homeowner to refinance the current note into a more favorable, new loan.

> The homeowner will be required to meet minimum guideline qualifications set by the loan program applicable to the refinance.

> The property value and condition will be scrutinized during the process.

The qualifications of the property and homeowner must meet the lender guidelines put in place to ensure that adequate security exists in the transaction.

In the past, refinance transactions were handled within the mainstream lending offices and typically followed the processes of a standard loan. If the loan is in default and has entered the stage where the loss mitigation department has become involved, modifications or exceptions to traditional lending guidelines may be required to enable the homeowner to refinance the loan.

Traditional refinance requirements include

- Adequate consumer credit history with no late payments for the prior 2-years

- A mortgage history that illustrates timely mortgage payments over the prior 2-year period

- Credit scores that meet or exceed the loan program minimum criteria

- No bankruptcy, NOD, or Foreclosure in the recent history

- Adequate employment history in the same line of work or profession for the previous two years

- High likelihood of continued employment income into the future

- Debt-to-Income ratios that fall within the specifications set by the lender to limit the incidence of mortgage default

- Property Value and/or homeowner investment sufficient to meet LTV requirements

- Acceptable property condition

The homeowner may qualify for a traditional refinance transaction if they have contacted you early in the process or before a default occurs on the loan.

> Example: A homeowner with an adjustable rate mortgage contacts the loss mitigation before or soon after the first rate adjustment occurs.
>
> The homeowner may know that the interest rate adjustment that will or has occurred on the loan will generate a new required payment that they cannot support over a long term.

If a homeowner appears to be a candidate for a traditional refinance, you should refer them to a loan officer within the lending institution where you conduct your loss mitigation activity or to a reputable mortgage loan officer who can screen the application package. The loan officer will be able to assess the ability of the homeowner to obtain a refinance.

You can gain a basic understanding of the elements that the loan officer will scrutinize by understanding the product or guideline matrix used within the traditional lending arena.

Guideline Matrix

A guideline matrix is a chart that dictates the

- approval requirements

- underwriting basis

- specific approval terms

of each loan product that you a homeowner might use to obtain a refinance on the property.

You should view the matrix as a snapshot of the full underwriting guidelines that will be applied to the homeowner. This will assist you in making a determination as to whether you should continue the loss mitigation process, refer the homeowner to a traditional lender, or short refinance department for assessment. If the homeowner qualifies for a general refinance or short refinance, the remaining loss mitigation efforts may not be necessary.

You will use this tool in relationship to homeowners who have

- An adequate equity position in the property

  an equity position is illustrated by comparing the loan amount necessary with the value of the property (LTV). The theory behind the LTV is that the higher the equity in the property, the less likely a homeowner is to default

- A credit history that illustrates the ability to meet minimum lender requirements

  The guidelines for what is an acceptable credit history will vary depending on the lender and the loan type. A common requirement is that the homeowner must have a 2-year history with minimal credit blemishes. The chapter relating to understanding credit will provide you with additional insight into the rating of a credit history.

- An employment history that illustrates the ability to meet the minimum lender requirements

  The guidelines for what is an acceptable employment history will vary depending on the lender and the loan type. A common requirement is that the homeowner must have a 2-year history of employment within the same line of work or profession. A homeowner who cannot meet this requirement may still receive a refinance loan if sufficient explanation regarding the lack of history and proof regarding the likelihood of future employment can be provided.

- Debt to Income (DTI) Ratios that will fall below the standards of the refinance loan limitations

  DTI Ratio on the property only of 29% or less and DTI Ratio for all open debt of 41% or less

  The chapter relating to DTI Calculations will provide you with additional insight into the methods employed to calculate debt ratios.

The traditional refinance option is typically employed with those homeowners who contact the loss mitigation department before a default situation exists. These homeowners are aware of potential payment stability issues before they begin to occur and may contact you to assist them in obtaining assistance to minimize the risk of default.

If the homeowner cannot qualify for a traditional refinance, other loss mitigation options may be employed to cure the default. One such option is the short refinance.

A short refinance may enable a homeowner who has a lower equity position to obtain a refinance through the lender with whom you work or who is holding the note that is in default. The principal balance refinanced in these transactions will be lowered to meet the current market value of the property as set by an appraiser and may enable some homeowners to maintain the property

The HOPE or FHA Secure loans may provide some homeowners who have multiple issues relating to the file to obtain a governmentally assisted refinance loan

Regardless of the source of the refinance loan, the loss mitigation specialist should gain the ability to review matrix and determine whether a homeowner's package will fall within the traditional refinance matrix, HOPE, FHA Secure, other Government Program, or the short refinance matrix. An understanding of the guideline matrix applied to loan products will enable you to determine

- whether referral for a short refinance or a traditional refinance might be available for the homeowner

- what proofs and documentation the homeowner may need to supply during the application process

- whether you should proceed with the most effective loss mitigation strategy if the homeowner is not in a position to qualify for a short, government, or traditional refinance

Each program will have product matrix available. These matrixes are a snapshot of the minimum requirements needed to place a loan in a particular approval tier or level. The internal guidelines or underwriting requirements will contain additional or expansion requirements that pertain to each sub-element of the matrix. In the loss mitigation process, the guideline matrix should be considered as an assessment tool to determine if the homeowner has the potential for a refinance, not as a pre-qualification for the refinance. Only a qualified loan officer or mortgage broker acting on behalf of the mortgage lender can pre-qualify the homeowner. As the loss mitigation specialist, you can screen for the likelihood of a loan.

Approval guidelines should not be confused with proper documentation. Most approval guidelines are based on your homeowner's credit and debt ratios. To complete an assessment of possible refinance transactions for the homeowner, you will need to complete two practice forms. These forms are:

Credit Scoring

Debt-to-Income Ratio

You should locate these two forms in the correct area of the workbook and use them for this section of the course. If you have not yet completed the practice lessons, you will need to do so now.

SAMPLE PRODUCT MATRIX

Credit Grade	Credit Score	Mortgage History	Consumer History	Bankruptcy/ Foreclosure	Maximum Debt Ratio	Maximum LTV	Maximum CLTV
A	660+	0x30	1x30	3/3	41%	97%	97%
A-	620-669	1x30	2x30	3/3	45%	95%	97%
B	590-619	2x30	1x60	2/2	47%	90%	95%
B-	560-589	1x60	2x60	2/2	50%	85%	95%
C	540-559	2x60	1x90	1/1	50%	80%	90%
C-	520-539	1x90	2x90	1/1	55%	75%	90%
D	490-519	2x90	3x90	>1 year	55%	70%	85%

Figure 4:1 Sample Product Matrix
This form is included for reference purposes only. You should obtain the applicable HUD or Lender forms for use in a negotiation.

Matrix Definitions

Credit Grade The credit grade is an internal naming system for the different approval levels and relates to the components of the homeowners file as well as the type of loan program that may be available for the homeowner.

Credit Score The credit score refers to the score considered most applicable by the lender. Some lenders use the most regionally appropriate of the three credit bureau scores while others take the middle of the three scores for qualification purposes.

Details relating to the credit score, the methods applied to scoring, and the use of credit scores by the lender is included later in the coursework

Mortgage History The mortgage history referenced by the lender typically relates to the mortgage of the primary residence. Most loss mitigation negotiations will be related to the primary residence.

Most grading uses the maximum mortgage late payments and does not consider the lower late pays as part of the grading process.

Example: 1x60 negates the use of all 30-day late payments

The period of assessment for the mortgage history will vary depending on the lender. Some will assess only the last 12-month period while others may assess the last 24-month period. The assessment term will often be included within the guideline short sheet available from the lender.

Consumer History The consumer history is rated by following the same practices as with the mortgage history except you will apply the rating methods to the consumer credit illustrated on the report.

A mortgage loan relating to a property that is not a primary residence of the homeowner will often be rated as a consumer loan.

Foreclosure and Bankruptcy

Many traditional lenders will require that any foreclosure or bankruptcy that the consumer underwent be seasoned. Seasoning means to age or that the matter occurred a specified amount of time in the past.

Debt Ratio

Details relating to the inclusions and calculations of the DTI Ratio are included later in the coursework. You should gain the ability to calculate various applications of the DTI Ratio.

Maximum debt ratio limitations will vary depending on the transaction and potential lender.

LTV

The LTV is the Loan to Value Ratio. The maximum LTV that a homeowner can receive from the lender is based on the quality of the homeowners file. The common theory behind the LTV is that the higher the amount of equity the homeowner has in the property the less likely they are to default on the loan. The secondary theory is that the lower the LTV position, the higher the security the lender will have in the event the homeowner does default and the property must be sold through surrender loss mitigation options.

The ability to calculate the loan amount that may be received by the homeowner is important elements to the prescreening for certain refinance loan possibilities.

To calculate the LTV

Value	x	Percentage	=	LTV

Example:

Appraised Property Value:	$100,000
Maximum LTV	x .80
Maximum Refinance Loan	$ 80,000

The LTV must be sufficient to cover the mortgage debt owed against the property, any fees, and costs relating to the refinance transaction, and possibly any subordinate liens that exist against the property.

CLTV

Some lenders may provide a percentage figure termed a CLTV (Combined Loan-To-Value). A combined loan to value is the total amount of debt allowed to be outstanding against the property and still complete the transaction.

The CLTV is used more often in purchase transactions, but may apply to a refinance if subordinate liens exist that must be paid off before the refinance transaction or other debt must be consolidated to ensure the homeowner meets DTI requirements.

The calculation of the CLTV is completed using the same processes, as the LTV ratio except you will substitute the LTV percentage for the CLTV difference illustrated within the matrix.

This matrix is for example purposes only. Each loan program will have specific guidelines and approval levels. You should refer to the loss mitigation manual provided by the lender with whom your work or discuss the file with a reputable lender in your area for approval guidelines for your particular homeowner's file.

GRADING

- To begin the grading processes use your Credit Report Scoring key and DTI Ratio Form to find the correct placement of your homeowner.

- Start with the highest level on the product matrix. (Example 'A')

- Compare each decision factor in your homeowner's profile with the minimum guidelines.

- If you homeowner does not meet eligibility requirements for the level, move to the next lowest approval level

- Continue the process until your homeowner places within each criteria maximum for that approval level.

Example:

Item	Homeowner	1st Matrix Level Approval
Credit Score	589	B-
Mortgage History	0x30	A

Consumer History	1x60	B
Bankruptcy	None	A
Foreclosure	None	A
Debt Ratio	43%	A-

Using the example criteria included above and the sample product matrix included in the preceding page, the homeowner would qualify for an approval rating of B or a B-.

It is possible that the lender will refinance the transaction so the next step is to present your homeowner with the possibility of a refinance transaction instead of loss mitigation.

The homeowner will then need to determine if the property value is within the LTV approval rating. A loan officer within the lending institution holding the mortgage note that may enter default will be able to assist you in completing additional screening.

If both the homeowner and property qualify, a refinance transaction would be a better option than many loss mitigation techniques. You should always explore the refinance options before proceeding with more intensive loss mitigation assessments.

SHORT REFINANCE

If the homeowner profile meets the qualifying criteria included on the lender holding the defaulted mortgage note, but the property does not meet the qualifications, the potential for a short refinance exists. The guideline matrix for a short refinance will typically not be as strict regarding the homeowner's credit history, as many homeowners who are seeking this type of relief will already have an extensive mortgage default history.

Some lenders do not offer a short refinance loss mitigation options but include this element of the loss mitigation process as a component of the loan modification.

The short refinance dictates that the homeowner meet the minimum qualification requirements set forth for the lenders short refinance loan program.

The short refinance often relates to a property whose market value has fallen due to present market conditions. This drop in value creates a scenario where the value of the property is less than the amount owed on the note.

Some lenders will reduce the principal amount owed on the note and provide the homeowner with a refinance transaction if all elements of their file indicate a high likelihood that the actions will result in stable future payments by the homeowner.

Some lenders will consider the short refinance only after all other loss mitigation efforts up to the deed in lieu of foreclosure have failed.

If the lender holding the note of the homeowner you are working with is willing to consider a short refinance option, you should be able to scrutinize the guideline matrix in the same manner that you would for a traditional refinance.

The possibility of a refinance transaction presents the homeowner with an alternative to many, more intensive, loss mitigation options. It is important that you screen each potential loss mitigation file to determine if the possibility of a refinance or short refinance exists.

The traditional refinance typically falls above (better than) any loss mitigation option on the intervention rating scale.

The short refinance typically falls below (worse than) the loan modification option from the perspective of the lender. The short sale may actually fall below (worse than) short sale options in the lender's viewpoint because the lender may receive the same amount of money in a short refinance as they would in a short sale, but the lender will be working with a homeowner who has a history of default.

The Government Loan option such as the HOPE loan will be categorized as better or worse then other options based on the opinion of the homeowner. Any homeowner who desires a review by the HOPE program or other governmentally underwritten loan program designed to provide relief for defaulted homeowners should be encouraged to do so. HUD provides enhanced regulations and timelines pertaining to loss mitigation and it is important that the homeowner, loss mitigation specialist, and the lender follow these timelines.

The loan officer or mortgage broker working on behalf of the lender who will fund the loan will complete the loan application package and the gather of the required documentation.

The loss mitigation specialist should gain the ability to conduct pre-screening activity to determine if the possibility of a refinance transaction applies to the homeowner but should not enter into the completion of a refinance application package unless they are also trained as a loan officer.

CONVENTIONAL LOAN UNDERWRITING GUIDELINES

		MANUAL UNDERWRITING	AUTOMATED UNDERWRITING
ELIGIBILITY	Programs	30-Year Fixed, 40-Year Fixed, 35-Year Interest Only	30-Year Fixed, 40-Year Fixed, 35-Year Interest Only
	Loan Purpose	Purchase Transactions Only	
	Occupancy Status	Owner-Occupied Primary Residence Only	
	LTV / CLTV Limits	Maximum LTV 100%, Maximum CLTV 107% (90% Maximum LTV/CLTV on Manufactured Housing on 30 and 40-year only. Manufactured housing is NOT permitted on interest only	
CREDIT	Minimum Contribution	None Required	
	Minimum Credit Score	620 (regardless of automated underwriting findings)	None Required
	Alternative Credit	Permitted. Minimum of four sources with a twelve month satisfactory payment record. One of the sources must be a twelve month VOR	(regardless of automated underwriting findings)
	BK / NOD / Foreclosure	Minimum 3 years since discharge/sale date and evidence of reestablished credit required	Determined by automated approval
	Collections	If individual account balance is less than $250 or the total of all such accounts is $1000 or less not required to pay at closing.	Determined by automated approval
	Student Loan	Must not be in default. Deferred allowed as long as payment calculated in debt ratios	
RATIOS & INCOME	Back End Ratio	45% (35-Year Interest Only qualified as 35-Year fully amortized)	55% regardless of underwriting findings
	Temporary Buy downs	Temporary buy downs allowed on 30-Year & 40-Year Fixed Rate loans only. No buy downs permitted on Interest Only. LTV > 95% qualify at note rate. LTV < or = 95% qualify at buy down + 1	Determined by automated approval
	Non-Occupancy Co-Signor	Permitted on 30-Year & 40-Year Fixed rate loans only with LTV , or = 90%. Occupant borrower(s) total debt ratio max 55%, combined max 45%	
	Boarder Income	None Permitted	
	PT / OT / 2nd Job / Bonus Income	Permitted with a minimum 12 month history	Determined by automated approval
PROPERTY	Eligible Property Types	Single family (no in laws suites/ granny flats) 5 acres maximum. Condominiums must meet FNMA Condominium Project Acceptance Policy or be FHA Approved PUD. Manufactured Housing – limited to 90% LTV/CLTV with 10% down payment from borrower's own funds on 30 and 40-year	
	Appraisals	One of the following appraisal forms is required: Uniform Residential Appraisal Report (URAR) Fannie Mae/Freddie Mac for 1004 (Single Family / PUD) Form 1004C (Manufactured Home Appraisal Report) Form 1073 (Individual Condominium Appraisal Report)	
FUNDS TO CLOSE	Minimum Down Payment	No minimum down payment required except for manufactured home loans which require 10% borrowers own funds	Determined by automated approval
	Cash Reserves	1 month	
	Gift Funds	Permitted. No Maximum. May be used to supplement cash reserves.	
	Seller Contribution	Contributions by any interested party towards recurring and/or non-recurring closing costs are limited to: 3% of the purchase price if LTV is > 90% 6% of the purchase price if LTV is < or = 90% Any contribution exceeding these limits requires a downward adjustment to the sales price to reflect the amount that exceeds the limits	
MORTGAGE INSURANCE	Monthly Mortgage Insurance	Required on all loans with an LTV > 80%	

Mortgage Insurance Rates

30-Year Fixed / 40-Year Fixed / 35-Year IOP (non-conforming loan)

LTV	Coverage	Pricing
95.01 – 100	35%	.85
90.01 – 95	35%	.75
85.01 – 90	35%	.55
80.01 – 95	35%	.41

35-Year IOP (conforming loan)

LTV	Coverage	Pricing
97.01 – 100	20%	.59
95.01 – 97	18%	.50
90.01 – 95	16%	.46
85.01 – 90	12%	.34
80.01 – 95	6%	.23

4:2 Sample: Lender Supplied Guideline Matrix This form is included for reference purposes only. You should obtain the applicable HUD or Lender forms for use in negotiation.

CHAPTER

5

Short Sale

The lender and the homeowner may agree to place the house for sale within the general real estate market. This is often termed a short sale or preforeclosure sale.

To facilitate the sale in today's economy, the lender will often need to reduce the principal balance required to pay off the note. This reduction is the origin of the term 'short'. The reduction helps to increase the interest of potential buyers and helps to facilitate the sale of the property.

A short sale is sometimes termed a Pre-Foreclosure Sale (PFS). The short sale is a benefit to the homeowner because they have an entry on the credit report of less severity than a foreclosure detail. The short sale is the first level of the property surrender loss mitigation negotiations. The loss mitigation specialist should screen for any property retention options before considering a short sale assessment if the homeowner is willing to work toward keeping their home.

The pre-foreclosure loss mitigation process enables the homeowner to relinquish the property and negotiate to remove any accountability for any sale shortfalls that may result from the sale of the property in the current market.

- In a pre-foreclosure sale, the lender agrees to accept the proceeds of a sale set a current fair market value as indicated by comparables and appraisals for the market of the property.

- Upon receiving an approved sales price from the lender, the homeowner will place the home for sale in the market.

- The homebuyer is responsible for facilitating the showing, offers, and ultimate sale of the property.

- Upon the acceptance and closing of a suitable offer, the lender provides a mortgage satisfaction to the original homeowner listed on the mortgage note.

- This satisfaction will be provided even when additional sums of money were due under the note between the original homeowner and the mortgage lender.

If the lender is willing to negotiate the short sale terms with the homeowner and a buyer can be found to meet the negotiated terms, the homeowner avoids the foreclosure process.

If the property was insured through FHA, VA or another entity and the lender has followed all of the required procedures, the lender may be entitled to recoup all or some of the loss incurred through the short sale discount process from the insurer.

Appropriateness of Short Sale Offerings

The short sale option is most frequently used for homeowners who have failed to meet the qualifications necessary for any of the home retention loss mitigation plans.

The home surrender loss mitigation strategy that has the lowest long-term negative impact on the homeowner is the short sale. The short sale offering should be given to homebuyers who have failed to meet the criteria of lesser loss mitigation workouts or who have illustrated a lack of desire in retaining the property.

The lack of desire in retaining the property does create additional verification requirements of the loss mitigation specialist. Most lenders will refuse to consider loss mitigation negotiations with a homeowner who is making a decision to surrender the property based on a desire to 'walk away' from the transaction rather than one who requires loss mitigation intercession due to a financial hardship.

The short sale negotiation is appropriate for homeowners who illustrate certain characteristics.

- The homeowner who is clearly unable to pay their mortgage obligation but is willing to work with the lender to bring the negotiation to an acceptable conclusion

- The property value is less than the amount owed against the note or is located an area where current market offerings for property of similar size, construction and location is being offered for sale at a price below the amount of the mortgage

- The negotiations and interview with he homebuyer have illustrated that other alternatives such as forbearance, loan modification, or refinance are not options given the homeowner situation

- Special consideration for a short sale authorization may be given if there is a verifiable reason why the homeowner must vacate the property and at least one of the common criteria common to the short sale appropriateness survey apply to the situation.

    A verifiable reason to vacate the property could include

    - Job Transfer
    - Divorce
    - Reduced Income
    - Death of One Party

As the loss mitigation specialist, it will be a part of your function to scrutinize the homeowner's position to ensure that any options offered during the negotiation processes are necessary.

Some buyer's may choose to walk away from their mortgage even though they have the capability to make the monthly payments required under the note.

This decision on the part of the homebuyer may occur for a variety of reasons including

- A desire to relocate

- Lower property values appreciation than expected

- Decline of a neighborhood

- Other reasons specific to the homeowner

It is especially important that the homeowner's situation and need for intervention be documented if the lender plans to submit a request to the mortgage insurer for financial payment to offset the loss incurred during the short sale property.

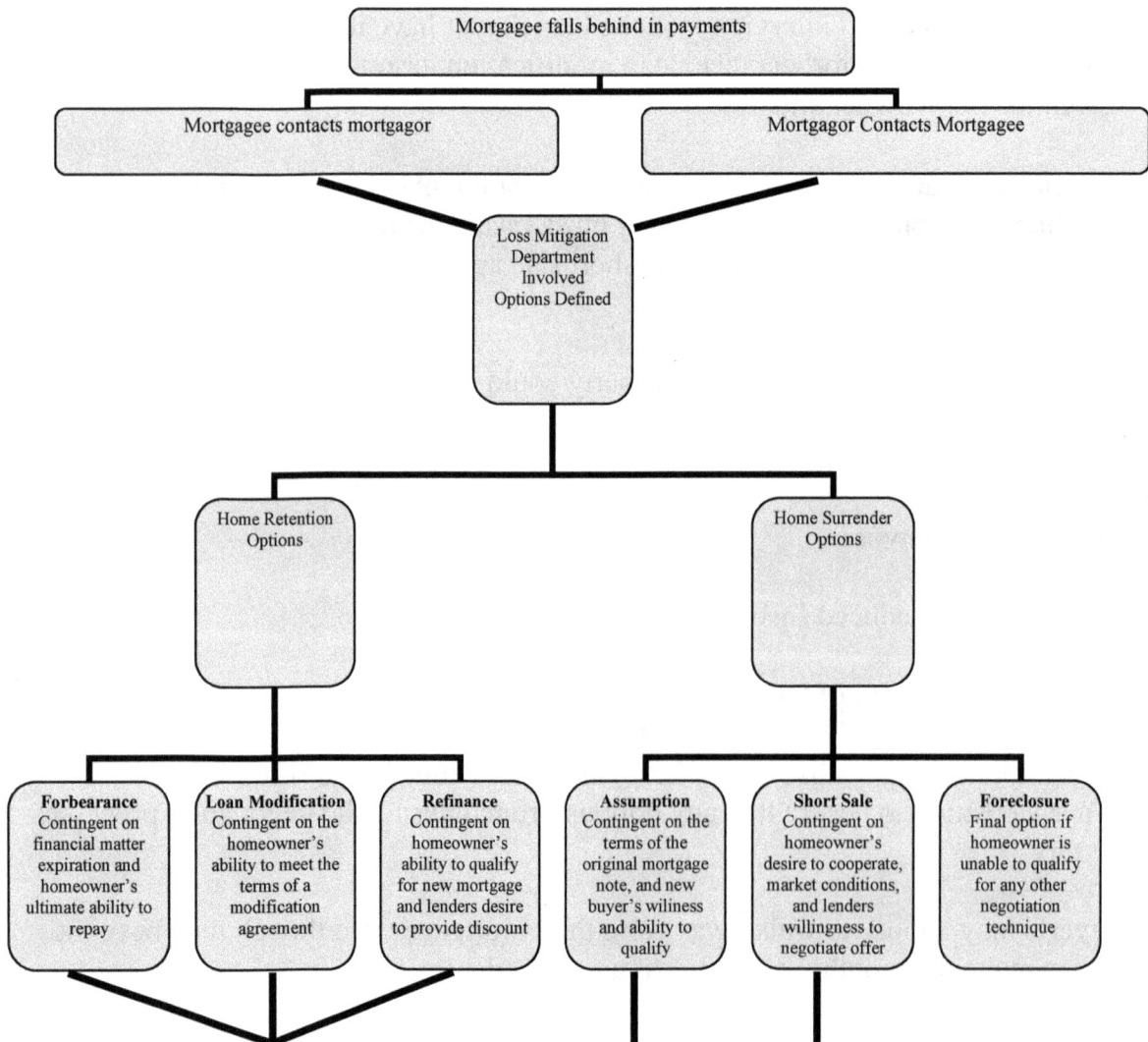

```
                    ┌─────────────────────────────────┐
                    │ Mortgagee falls behind in payments│
                    └─────────────────────────────────┘
              ┌──────────────────────┐      ┌──────────────────────────┐
              │ Mortgagee contacts   │      │ Mortgagor Contacts       │
              │ mortgagor            │      │ Mortgagee                │
              └──────────────────────┘      └──────────────────────────┘
                            ┌─────────────────────┐
                            │ Loss Mitigation     │
                            │ Department          │
                            │ Involved            │
                            │ Options Defined     │
                            └─────────────────────┘
              ┌─────────────────┐              ┌─────────────────┐
              │ Home Retention  │              │ Home Surrender  │
              │ Options         │              │ Options         │
              └─────────────────┘              └─────────────────┘
```

Forbearance	Loan Modification	Refinance	Assumption	Short Sale	Foreclosure
Contingent on financial matter expiration and homeowner's ultimate ability to repay	Contingent on the homeowner's ability to meet the terms of a modification agreement	Contingent on homeowner's ability to qualify for new mortgage and lenders desire to provide discount	Contingent on the terms of the original mortgage note, and new buyer's wiliness and ability to qualify	Contingent on homeowner's desire to cooperate, market conditions, and lenders willingness to negotiate offer	Final option if homeowner is unable to qualify for any other negotiation technique

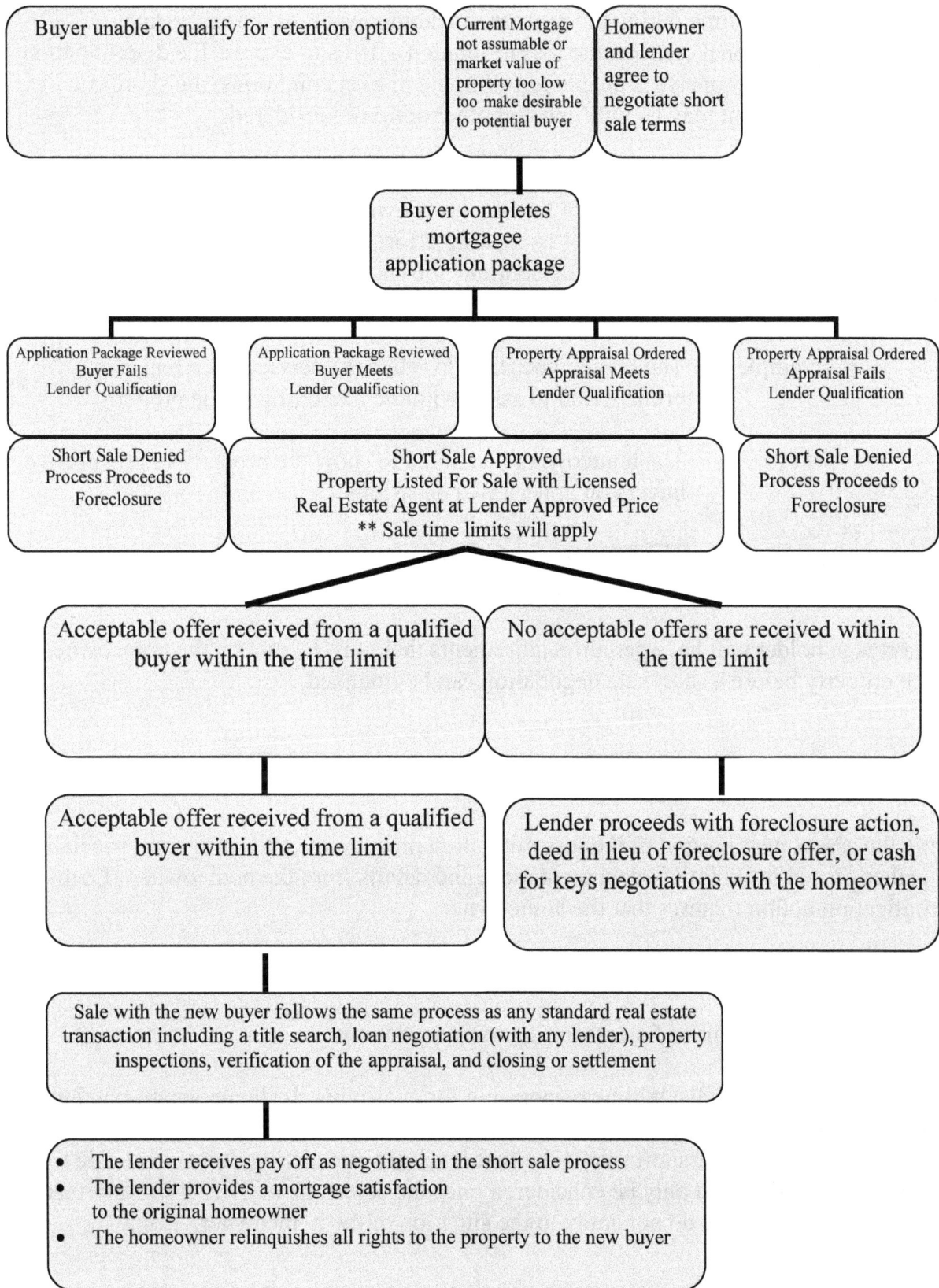

```
┌─────────────────────────────────────────┐  ┌──────────────┐  ┌──────────────┐
│ Buyer unable to qualify for retention     │  │ Current      │  │ Homeowner    │
│ options                                    │  │ Mortgage     │  │ and lender   │
│                                            │  │ not assumable│  │ agree to     │
│                                            │  │ or market    │  │ negotiate    │
│                                            │  │ value of     │  │ short        │
│                                            │  │ property too │  │ sale terms   │
│                                            │  │ low too make │  │              │
│                                            │  │ desirable to │  │              │
│                                            │  │ potential    │  │              │
│                                            │  │ buyer        │  │              │
└─────────────────────────────────────────┘  └──────────────┘  └──────────────┘
```

Buyer completes mortgagee application package

| Application Package Reviewed Buyer Fails Lender Qualification | Application Package Reviewed Buyer Meets Lender Qualification | Property Appraisal Ordered Appraisal Meets Lender Qualification | Property Appraisal Ordered Appraisal Fails Lender Qualification |

| Short Sale Denied Process Proceeds to Foreclosure | Short Sale Approved Property Listed For Sale with Licensed Real Estate Agent at Lender Approved Price ** Sale time limits will apply | Short Sale Denied Process Proceeds to Foreclosure |

Acceptable offer received from a qualified buyer within the time limit

No acceptable offers are received within the time limit

Acceptable offer received from a qualified buyer within the time limit

Lender proceeds with foreclosure action, deed in lieu of foreclosure offer, or cash for keys negotiations with the homeowner

Sale with the new buyer follows the same process as any standard real estate transaction including a title search, loan negotiation (with any lender), property inspections, verification of the appraisal, and closing or settlement

- The lender receives pay off as negotiated in the short sale process
- The lender provides a mortgage satisfaction to the original homeowner
- The homeowner relinquishes all rights to the property to the new buyer

NOTE: If at any time during the process, the homeowner, or the real estate professional contacts the loss mitigation offices to express the determination that the property is unable to sell in the market conditions, the short sale agreement may be nullified and other options considered.

NOTE: The homeowner must show a good faith effort to sell the property. If at any time, it becomes apparent that the homeowner is not cooperating with the real estate professional or expending effort to assist with marketing the home, the lender will typically discontinue the short sale agreement and proceed with other options to regain the property.

Example: The homeowner fails to retain the services of a real estate professional to assist with the marketing of the property

The homeowner has failed to show the property to prospective buyers on at least two occasions

The homeowner fails to complete basic maintenance on the property placing the marketability and value at risk

The mortgage holder will have certain requirements that must be met by the homeowner and the property before a short sale negotiation can be finalized.

Qualification

During the assessment portion of the loss mitigation process, the loss mitigation specialist will gather certain information, documentation, and details from the homeowner. Each loss mitigation option requires that the homeowner

- Meet the qualifications set forth by the lender

- Verify the need for loss mitigation negotiations

The loss mitigation specialist will be responsible for qualifying the homeowner, obtaining verification, and planning the negotiation package for remittal to the lender or loss mitigation supervisor. The short sale is the first level of surrender workouts available to the homeowner and should only be considered once the screening activity illustrates that retention work out options do not apply to the situation of the homeowner. If the homeowner does not meet the short sale qualifications set forth by the lender, the loss review supervisor will decline the short sale offer.

Income The homeowner must illustrate that a financial need exists that makes the likelihood of curing the default through other, lesser loss mitigation options unlikely.

- An unexpected decreased in income

- Proof than the property is of limited value or marketability

- That they are currently in default on the mortgage debt

Assessments The homeowner must be able to verify that their personal situation has been assessed to determine if any lesser loss mitigation options may be suitable before some lenders will consider the short sale offer.

You should review all of the assessment elements of the previous chapters to ensure that you have an understanding of the lesser options before proceeding with the short sale negotiations. If any lesser workout may apply to the homeowner, you should present these options before assisting the homeowner in completing a short sale offer.

Occupancy Most lenders will require that property be an owner occupied primary residence.

Second homes, vacation homes, investment property, and other non-owner occupied property will typically result in a lender decline of the short sale negotiation request.

Many lenders will have screened the intended occupancy of the property at the time that that the original mortgage loan was granted. The lender may review the statements of the homeowner on the original mortgage application and review the occupancy declaration that was completed during the closing of the original mortgage loan.

It is important that the loss mitigation specialist ask the homeowner about the contents of these documents during the analysis portion of the loss mitigation process.

If any questionable entries may exist on these documents, the inclusions will need to be addressed before most lenders will approve a loss mitigation package.

Property Value   The lender may require that an appraisal be completed on the property to illustrate that there is a sufficient drop in market value below the note amount to make lesser loss mitigation options impossible.

Example: The lender requires that the current market value of the property be equal to or less than 63% of the outstanding principal balance on the mortgage.

Principal Balance Owed	$228,976
	X .63
Maximum Appraised Value	$144,254
Actual Appraised Value	$135,600

The lender will require that this appraisal illustrate that the value of the property is substantially less than the amount of the outstanding mortgage against the property. The example above would illustrate an appraised value that meets the minimum requirements of the lender.

The appraised value will also dictate the acceptable minimum list price for the property if the short sale negotiations proceed to offering the property for sale.

The lender will order a URAR – Uniform Residential Appraisal to determine the market value of the property.

A copy of the appraisal will be provided to the homeowner.

The homeowner and the lender will use this appraisal as a baseline for negotiations as to the minimum purchase offer that will be accepted the lender.

An offer at or above the minimum acceptable offer could enable the homeowner to receive a satisfaction of the mortgage note.

An offer below the minimum acceptable amount negotiated between the homeowner and the lender may be declined or may require that the homeowner pay any deficit funds required by the negotiations.

Property Condition

The homeowner typically completes cosmetic repairs necessary to maintain and market the property. Cosmetic repairs will fall within the requirement of general maintenance or the homeowner's visible efforts to market the property.

If the appraisal, statements of the homeowner, or other inspection show that more elaborate repairs are necessary at the property, these may need to be addressed before a new buyer can receive a mortgage loan against the property.

Lenders will often reject a short sale offering if it is illustrated that the cost of repairs exceeds a specified percentage of the value of the property.

Many guidelines stipulate that the repair cost may not exceed 10% of the "repaired appraised value".

Other options may apply that will enable the continuance of short sale negotiations.

- If extensive and/or costly repairs are necessary at the property and the cost of these repairs is within the homeowner's ability to pay, the homeowner should address these repairs as part of the efforts to improve the marketability of the property.

- If extensive and/or costly repairs are necessary at the subject property and the cost of these repairs are beyond the ability of the homeowner to pay, the repairs may be delayed to see if the repairs can be addressed under a valid offer from a buyer.

If the offer from a viable buyer is above the minimum sales price agreed upon by the lender, the funds to complete the necessary repairs might be allocated from sale proceeds. The ability to allocate these funds may be contingent on minimum profit requirements of any insurer involved in the lenders negotiations.

If the offer from a viable offer is equal to the minimum amount required by the lender the homeowner and the new buyer might be required to work out the allocation of the repair costs within the contract.

> If the homeowner and the buyer cannot agree to the cost allocation of the necessary repairs, the offer from the buyer will be declined.

- If the offer from a viable buyer is received but the cost of the repairs will result in a proceeds shortfall unacceptable to the lender, the lender may decline the offer or the new buyer may opt to complete the repairs using their own funds.

- In rare circumstances, the lender may agree to pay the costs of the repairs if a viable offer is received from a buyer but the repair costs become the one element that will cause the deal to fall through.

Title Search

The lender will typically require that all subordinate liens against the property be discharged or released before the short sale approved price can be finalized.

The mortgage holder will order a title search as a part of the processing stage of the short sale negotiation. If the title search uncovers junior liens or other encumbrances, the short sale may proceed as planned if discharge arrangements can be made.

> Pay Off   The homeowner may pay all or a portion of the liens

The mortgage holder may agree to pay a portion of the liens from a part of the sale proceeds

Price Increase The mortgage holder and homebuyer may agree to attempt to facilitate a sale at a higher price to increase the sale proceeds by the shortfall necessary to pay of the liens

NOTE: Junior liens may be negotiated for a short payoff

If the liens against the property are such that satisfactory payment agreements cannot be reached, the short sale negotiations will halt and the lender will proceed to pursue other options.

Duration   The loss mitigation specialist will assist in the negotiation of the term provided for the sale of the property.

The negotiations should be based on the likelihood of a sale within a set time based on

> market conditions

> property condition

> sales price

> any other information deemed applicable

The time allocation allowed for the sale will vary by market but is often set at a three to six month period.

If at the expiration of the negotiated term, the homeowner can illustrate a high likelihood of a sale in the near future through a sales contract or by other means the period may be extended.

Termination   Either party may terminate the short sale agreement at any time during the term. Common termination causes include

- Title matters, including subordinate liens that cannot be discharged or cleared to facilitate a sale

- A lack of good faith effort on the part of the homeowner to facilitate the sale through marketing effort, property maintenance or other means

- If it becomes obvious through lack of buyer interest that the property will not sell during the negotiated short sale term, the buyer and lender may consider other alternatives

The buyer may voluntarily withdraw from the program at any time

The lender will be bound by the negotiation agreement unless the buyer fails to show good faith or the title search reveals matters that cannot be corrected to create a clear and marketable title.

Agreement   A written agreement detailing all of the negotiated points must be executed between the lender and the homeowner. This agreement will define

- Define end date for marketing

- State the minimum acceptable net proceeds

- Define the methods of termination of agreement

- Outline the homeowner good faith responsibilities

- State that failure to comply may result in foreclosure

- State that the receipt and closing of an acceptable offer will result in a satisfaction of the original note

Approval   Lenders may accept any offer on the property that they deem viable. The loss mitigation office will be responsible for reviewing any offers.

If the property involves a governmentally insured loan for which the lender intends to file a claim, certain restrictions on the sales price accepted by the lender may apply.

Regulations will also affect the amount of commission allocated to the real estate agent, and seller assistance provided to the seller.

A common restriction on an offer would be that the offer must be at or above 82% of the appraised value indicated by the appraisal completed during the loss mitigation negotiation process.

Combination   The Short Sale may be negotiated as a stand-alone transaction or may be combined with other loss mitigation strategies.

Example: Short sale with a special term of forbearance during the marketing term

NOTE: HUD Insured Loans may have special requirements relating to the criteria, minimum values, negotiation percentages, processes, costs, and other matters. If you are negotiating a loss mitigation transaction that involves a HUD Insured Loan, please see the GOVERNMENTAL REQUIREMENTS before proceeding with the negotiation processes.

SHORT SALE (PFS) CHECKLIST

Homeowner: _____

Requirement	Verification (Date, Amount, Source of Information etc.)
1. Has the homeowner experienced a verifiable loss of income or increase in living expenses?	
2. Is the term of this loss of income or increased living expense temporary or long term?	

3. Length of expected hardship?	
4. Has the homeowner worked with a loss mitigation specialist to qualify for lesser/retention loss mitigation options?	
5. Why is a special forbearance not applicable?	
6. Why is a loan modification not applicable?	
7. Why is a short refinance not applicable?	
8. Is the property owner occupied?	
9. Is the owner occupied status verifiable by the original mortgage application or closing occupancy declaration?	
10. Did the homeowner receive the How to Avoid Foreclosure brochure or obtain the services of a loss mitigation specialist?	
11. Will the loan be at least 30 days delinquent when the transaction closes? (show number of days)	
12. Did the income analysis to determine the homeowner's current inability to pay the debt include:	
• A financial statement provided by the homeowner	
• A credit report	
• Income/Expense Verifications	

• Evidence the homeowner hardship is long-term	
• Evidence the homeowner does not qualify for lesser/retention work out options	
13. The homeowner's current DTI ratio	
14. The homeowner's expected DTI ratio	
15. Does an appraisal show that:	
• The AS IS value is less than the loan amount? (show Value)	
• The property is worth at least 63% of the unpaid principal balance. (show negative equity ratio)	
• sale proceeds will result in a loss of more than $1,000	
• The property is not seriously damaged.	
16. Has a title search been obtained indicating marketable title?	
17. Does the title search indicate that junior liens exist against the property?	
18. Can these liens be discharged?	
19. Can these liens be paid/negotiated?	
20. Does the short sale agreement, executed by the homeowner	
• Define end date for marketing	

• State the minimum acceptable net proceeds	
• Define the methods of termination of agreement	
• Outline the homeowner good faith responsibilities	
• Offer relief not available through a retention loss mitigation option	
• State that failure to comply may result in foreclosure	
• State that the receipt and closing of an acceptable offer will result in a satisfaction of the original note	
21. Do Net Sale proceeds equal or exceed 82% of As Is Value? (show %)	

Figure 5:1 Sample Short Sale Checklist
This form is included for reference purposes only. You should obtain the applicable HUD or Lender forms for use in a negotiation.

Assessment Inclusion Checklist

Hardship Verification Forms

- Existence

- Term

    A verifiable reason to vacate the property could include

    Job Transfer
    Divorce
    Reduced Income
    Death of One Party

Used to determine the need and applicability of the short sale

Analysis of Lesser Options

- Forbearance Analysis Forms
- Loan Modification Analysis Forms
- Refinance / Short Refinance Analysis Form

Used to confirm that the default cannot be cured through lesser loss mitigation options

Occupancy Status Verification

- At original mortgage application
- At original mortgage closing
- Present

Used to verify the ability to negotiate a short sale agreement under lender guidelines

DTI Assessment

- Present

Used to prove the need for short sale negotiations

Surplus Income Assessment

- Present

Used to determine the ability of the homeowner to address subordinate liens or property condition issues

Credit Report

Used to confirm existence / amount of subordinate liens

Used to establish DTI Ratio

Title Search

Used to confirm existence / amount of subordinate liens

Property Inspection / Appraisal

Used to establish value of the property

Used as a baseline for acceptable sales price negotiation

Used to determine potential sale proceed surpluses

Used to establish that the condition of the property meets minimum qualification requirements

Figure 6: - HUD Release – PFS Application to Participate

CHAPTER

6

Deed-in-Lieu of Foreclosure

The deed in lieu of foreclosure is an option when the homeowner has no other resource for negotiation and the lender must obtain the return of the property.

The homeowner will relinquish their interest in the property by providing a deed to the lender.

The lender will provide the homeowner with a release or satisfaction from all obligations of the mortgage.

This transaction will enable the homeowner to minimize the impact of the negotiations on their credit.

This transaction helps to limit the time investment, expense, and property deterioration of a standard foreclosure process.

The deed in lieu (DIL) of foreclosure is the last level of loss mitigation negotiation before the default proceeds to a foreclosure. The deed in lieu of foreclosure options should be considered only after it has become apparent that the homeowner will not qualify for any other loss mitigation option.

The DIL dictates that the homeowner will

- surrender possession of the property promptly

- provide the lender with a deed transferring any and all interest held by the homeowner

- leave the property in good, marketable condition

The DIL Negotiation dictates that in exchange for the surrender by the homeowner, the lender will

- provide a satisfaction of the mortgage note held against the property

- accept the property in the condition illustrated by the Pre-DIL inspection

- not assess any sale shortfalls against the homeowner

In some instances, the homeowner may counter the deed in lieu negotiations and request that the lender provide them with a sum of payment in exchange for the surrender of the property. Under these terms, the homeowner will typically agree to provide a benefit to the lender above the standard DIL transaction.

Example: The homeowner will complete necessary cosmetic, cleaning, and other actions to leave the property in exceptional condition.

The actions of the homeowner will help to facilitate a speedy sale for the lender post transfer.

In exchange for the extra effort, speedy action or other negotiated item above the standards of the DIL transaction, the lender or the representative retained by the lender will provide the homeowner with a payment at the time that the keys to the property and deed relinquishing rights the property be handed over by the homeowner.

QUALIFICATION

Many lenders will require that the homeowner illustrate a financial need before approving the deed of lieu of foreclosure.

Some lenders may require proof that the property value has fallen to a level that makes a potential sale for a high enough amount to pay the outstanding mortgage note unlikely.

The lender may require a report from a real estate professional or appraiser that indicates the market time in the property area is of an extended term and that the party is not likely to sell during a standard short sale negotiation.

Many lenders will also require that the homeowner make a good faith effort to qualify for the property retention options available to them through the loss mitigation process before they will consider a deed in lieu of foreclosure offer.

During the assessment portion of the loss mitigation process, the loss mitigation specialist will gather certain information, documentation, and details form the homeowner. The loss mitigation options present levels of intervention designed to enable the homeowner and lender to work out the default cure strategy that presents the least loss to the lender an the homeowner.

Each loss mitigation option requires that the homeowner

- Meet the qualifications set forth by the lender

- Verify the need for loss mitigation negotiations

The loss mitigation specialist will be responsible for qualifying the homeowner, obtaining verifications, and planning the negotiation package for remittal to the lender or loss mitigation supervisor. If the homeowner does not qualify for any lesser loss mitigation option, the only recourse presently available before a foreclosure is the DIL process.

The negotiation of a DIL agreement is completed in reverse. Rather than qualify the homeowner for the DIL, the loss mitigation specialist should work to determine the disqualification of all other, lesser, loss mitigation workout strategies before presenting the DIL option.

Verification

The negotiation package must provide verification of the lack of qualification for all lesser loss mitigation options. This verification will present the criteria of the lesser option and illustrate through documentation the reasons that these options are not applicable to the homeowner.

Financial Need

The buyer must illustrate that a financial hardship exists that makes the ability to meet current mortgage obligations impossible and that property retention loss mitigation negotiation options will not alleviate this hardship.

All lesser loss mitigation options should be explored before opening the potential for a deed in lieu of foreclosure.

The lender will typically decline any loss mitigation negotiation if it is obvious that the homeowner has the ability to pay the mortgage note but has opted against doing so.

> Homeowners may choose to forego making payments on a mortgage if market conditions have drastically reduced the potential market value of the property, if the property condition has deteriorated, or for other reasons. These homeowners are often termed walk always and lenders will often decline any loss mitigation efforts on behalf of these homeowners.

The lender will often defer any DIL negotiation package if the property value indicators illustrate the potential for qualification for lesser loss mitigation options. If the property value meets the standards of lesser options, the reason these are not a viable solution should be well defined within the presentation package.

Occupancy

Most lenders will consider a deed in lieu of foreclosure only on owner occupied property.

> If the property is the second home, vacation home, investment property or other property of the owner, the lender will often decline a deed in lieu negotiation offer.

Some lenders will make an exception to the occupancy requirement if the property owner can illustrate that the default occurrence is related to a verifiable financial hardship such as a job loss, substantial decrease in income, death of one owner, etc.

Property Condition and Value

The market value or condition of the property will usually not play a large role in the negotiation of a deed in lieu of foreclosure process.

The only recourse beyond deed in lieu of foreclosure for the loss mitigation department is the full foreclosure process. The foreclosure proceedings are costly, time consuming and result in the lender obtaining the property.

The lender will obtain property in its present condition and at its current market value so these factors do not play a role in the deed in lieu negotiations from the perspective of the lender.

Property condition and value may become a tool for the homeowner in a deed in lieu of foreclosure negotiation if these can be considered to be above average.

The property owner may use the enhanced value and/or excellent condition to negotiate for a cash for keys component of the deed in lieu loss mitigation process.

SPECIAL

Special property condition stipulations may be applied to the negotiation process if the property is located in a presently declared disaster area.

These special conditions currently apply only to those areas hit by a major catastrophe such as Alabama, Florida, Louisiana, Mississippi, and Texas.

The government has provided individual assistance to help offset the damages to homeowners who have a dwelling within these areas that is uninhabitable and will not be restored. These individuals may hold a loan that enables the deed in lieu of foreclosure qualifications to be waived.

Title Search

When negotiating a deed in lieu of foreclosure as part of your loss mitigation efforts it is important that you remember that any subordinate liens against the property are not removed through the deed from the homeowner.

The lender will often stipulate that a title search must illustrate marketable title. If subordinate liens or judgments that may be held against the property exist, the homeowner must take steps to remove these liens, or the negotiation of deed in lieu may be declined.

Pay Off   The homeowner may pay all or a portion of the liens

NOTE: Junior liens may be negotiated for a short payoff

If the liens against the property are such that satisfactory payment agreements cannot be reached, the deed in lieu of foreclosure negotiations will halt and the lender will proceed with a full foreclosure process.

During the foreclosure process, any junior lien holders will be notified of the proceedings and have the opportunity to assert their interest in the property.

If the subordinate lien holders fail to enter a plea during the foreclosure process, the subordinate liens will be discharged by the courts in favor of the mortgage holder.

Federal Liens and Real Estate Tax Liens do not follow these same guidelines.

Cash for keys

The timely surrender and condition of the property at surrender are becoming an important element in DIL transactions.

Homeowner's who are willing to surrender the property quickly and leave the premises in exceptional condition may have another negotiation option. This extra negotiation option is known as Cash for Keys.

A homeowner may negotiate the payment of a stipulated amount of cash from the lender in exchange for leaving the property in broom clean condition (as is standard for traditional property transfers) and for vacating the property in a timely manner.

It is becoming a frequent occurrence for homeowner to leave a property with

- preventable damages

- excess debris

- other matters that the lender must clear up prior to offering the property for sale

The cash for keys negotiation element is one preventative measure that the lender may employ to ensure that they receive the property in the best possible condition at the time that the homeowner vacates. This method of obtaining entry to the property assists the lender in minimizing the costs and time delay necessary to evict the homeowner from the residence and prepare the property for sale.

NOTE

HUD Insured Loans may have special requirements relating to the criteria, minimum values, negotiation percentages, processes, costs, and other matters. If you are negotiating a loss mitigation transaction that involves a HUD Insured Loan, please see the GOVERNMENTAL REQUIREMENTS before proceeding with the negotiation processes.

Agreement

Common elements necessary to finalize a deed in lieu of foreclosure transfer negotiation include

- Certification by the homeowner that the property is their primary residence

- Certification by the homeowner regarding any other property owned

- Certification by the homeowner regarding the physical condition of the property

- Itemization of the fixtures included with the property

- A specific transfer date

- Certification by the homeowner that they will convey the property on the transfer date free of any debris, personal property or other items that may negatively impact the marketability of the property

- Certification by the homeowner regarding the payment of subordinate liens, utility bills, property taxes and other items that may be due against the property

- Acknowledgement by the homeowner that the deed in lieu of foreclosure process may have tax ramifications

Closing Process   The homeowner will execute a special warranty deed transferring all interest to the lender and providing warranty that the homeowner has not incurred any liens against the property other than as disclosed during the negotiation process

The lender will provide a satisfaction of the original note against the property illustrating that the mortgage has been satisfied

NOTE: HUD Insured Loans may have special requirements relating to the criteria, minimum values, negotiation percentages, processes, costs, and other matters. If you are negotiating a DIL transaction that involves a HUD Insured Loan, please see the applicable regulations before proceeding with the negotiation processes.

DEED-IN-LIEU OF FORECLOSURE CHECKLIST

Homeowner: _____

Requirement	Verification (Date, Amount, Source of Information etc.)
1. Has the homeowner experienced a verifiable loss of income or increase in living expenses?	
2. Is the term of this loss of income or increased living expense temporary?	
3. Is the property owner occupied?	
4. Is the owner occupied status verifiable by the original mortgage application or closing occupancy declaration?	
5. If the property is other than owner occupied, what exceptions qualify this property for DIL negotiations?	
6. Did the homeowner receive the How to Avoid Foreclosure brochure or obtain the services of a loss mitigation specialist?	
7. Will the loan be at least 30 days delinquent when the special warranty deed is accepted?	
8. Did the income analysis to determine the homeowner's current inability to pay the debt include:	
• A financial statement provided by the homeowner	
• A credit report	
• Income/Expense Verifications	

• Evidence the homeowner hardship is long-term	
9. The homeowner's current DTI ratio	
10. A recent appraisal indicates the AS IS property value is	
11. If any portion of the property is rented, is occupied conveyance approved?	
12. Has a title search been obtained showing good and marketable title?	
13. If junior liens exist, will these be discharged prior to transfer?	
14. Does a written DIL agreement, executed by the homeowner:	
• Require the property to be vacant and free of personal property at conveyance?	
• Convey title via a special warranty deed?	
• Convey clear title free of junior liens?	
• Require the homeowner to pay utility bills to the date of conveyance?	
• Require the homeowner to pay HOA dues or other assessments?	
• Advise the homeowner to obtain the advice of a tax consultant?	
• State that failure to comply may result in foreclosure	
Figure 2:2 DIL File Checklist This form is included for reference purposes only. You should obtain the applicable HUD or Lender forms for use in a negotiation.	

CHAPTER

7

Initial Assessment

From the moment you first speak with a homeowner, you should be gathering information and planning how you will negotiate a potential work out option. As a loss mitigation specialist, information, and communication with the homeowner are your most valuable tool in planning a work out strategy.

Obtaining information is quite simple if you just get over the natural shyness of asking strangers for personal information. You will find that, as a professional, people will answer almost any question you ask. However, you must ask!

On the next page, you will find an "Assessment Questionnaire" that we recommend using for each homeowner. Most of your initial contacts will be over the telephone. If you have this form handy, preferably bound in a notebook, you will always be able to lead the conversation exactly where you, as the loss mitigation specialist need it to go.

The pre-approval questionnaire is your most important ally. Most of the information required when pre-certifying the homeowner's ability to qualify for a work out option is included in the questionnaire. In fact, much of the basic information that will be required for your final negotiation package is included. This allows you to pre-fill some information, subject to verification during the processing stage of the negotiation process.

Pre-filling saves time and allows you and the homeowner to focus on the workout options available.

It is important to note that the initial contact sets the tone for your entire relationship with these homeowners. The ability to refer to the form inclusions and keep the assessment interview on track allows you to focus on building a relationship with the homeowner that will increase the likelihood of a successful workout negotiation.

The primary goal of the loss mitigation specialist is to minimize the costs and impact of financial issues that affect a homeowner's ability to make their mortgage payments.

You will work with the homeowner to assess the

- Existence of a verifiable hardship

- Term of the hardship

- Expected hardship recovery status

- DTI Ratios

    Current

    Expected

- Surplus Income

    Current

    Expected

- Occupancy status of the property

- Status of the Title

- Condition of the Property

- Value of the Property (possible homeowner knowledge)

- Ratio of Value to Principal (possible homeowner knowledge)

Upon completion of the homeowner assessment, you will rate the ability of each element of the homeowners file to meet the guidelines of the applicable mitigation option set by the lender.

The base details surrounding the default will assist you in beginning the processes of working out a viable retention or speedy relinquishment plan.

You will obtain documentation that provides third party verification of each piece of information provided to you by the homeowner.

Whether your work for the lender or the homeowner, the ability to negotiate a successful loss mitigation solution is essential to your success. Statistics have proven that the earlier the loss mitigation specialist takes action on a file, the more effective the negotiations for all parties. By expending proactive efforts rather than reactive response, you maximize the likelihood that a retention work out can be negotiated. The earlier you insert your skills into the transaction the lower the losses that will be suffered by the parties.

Foreclosure Prevention – Loss Mitigation Specialist

Assessment Questionnaire Date: _____

Source: Homeowner Contact _____   Lender Referral _____   Other: _____

Homeowner Name: _____   Co-Homeowner Name: _____

Home Phone: _____   Other Phone: _____   Best time(s) to call: _____

Explanation of Default/Notes: _____
_____
_____
_____

DOB: _____ SSN: _____   DOB: _____ SSN: _____

May I run a credit report? ___ Yes ___ No   May I run a credit report? ___ Yes ___ No

Are you behind in any other debt? _____
_____

Property Address: _____

Is this your primary residence? ___ Yes ___ No   Have you lived there since the original purchase? ___ Yes ___ No ___

No. Yrs: ___   Current Value $_____   Value at Purchase $_____   Mortgage Balance $_____

Missed Payments #_____   Amount Each Payment $ _____   Partial Payments: _____

Have you discussed the situation with the lender?   ___ Yes ___ No   Results _____

Are you presently Employed? ___ Yes ___ No   Are you presently Employed? ___ Yes ___ No

If No Reason: _____   If No Reason: _____

   Term: _____   Term: _____

Employer: _____   Employer: _____

Address: _____   Address: _____

Phone: _____ No yrs. ___ Position: _____   Phone: _____ No yrs. ___ Position: _____

Explanation of Employment/Notes: _____
_____
_____
_____

Figure 7:1 Sample Assessment Form – Page 1
This form is included for reference purposes only. You should obtain the applicable HUD or Lender forms for use in a negotiation.

PRESENT Income   EXPECTED Income – Date _____

Homeowners Mthly $_____   Homeowners Mthly $_____

          Prev Year $_____

Co-Homeowners Mthly $_____   Co-Homeowners Mthly $_____

          Prev Year $_____

Other Income _____ $_____   Other Income _____ $_____

Other Income _____ $_____   Other Income _____ $_____

   Total Income Current $_____   Total Income Expected $_____

PRESENT Debt

Mortgage $_____   Mortgage $_____

Auto 1 $_____   Auto 1 $_____

Auto 2 $_____   Auto 2 $_____

Revolving 1 $_____   Revolving 1 $_____

Revolving 2 $_____   Revolving 2 $_____

Other _____ $_____   Other _____ $_____

Other _____ $_____   Other _____ $_____

   Total Debt Current $_____   Total Debt Expected $_____

    Present DTI% _____   Expected DTI % _____ (current mortgage)

Analysis:

Current DTI _____   Expected DTI _____   Date _____   Notes: _____

Surplus Income Current   _____   Surplus Income Future   _____

Current Default # Days   _____   Current Default Base Amount _____

Owner Occ ___ Yes ___ No If No Exception Reason   _____

Est Payoff _____ Orig Mtg _____   Orig Value_____ Est Value _____

Forbearance Analysis: Term of Hardship _____   Current DTI _____   Expected DTI _____

      Surplus Income Present _____   Surplus Income Present _____

      Required Term _____   Forbearance Pmt Amt _____

      Post Forbearance Pmt Add On_____

Figure 7:2 Sample Assessment Form – Page 2
This form is included for reference purposes only. You should obtain the applicable HUD or Lender forms for use in a negotiation.

Modification Analysis:

Rate Change #1 _____   New Pmt _____   DTI _____

Rate Change #2 _____   New Pmt _____   DTI _____

Rate #1 + Term Mod 30   New Pmt _____   Rate #2 + Term Mod 40   New Pmt _____

Possible Principal Reduction   _____

Red + Rate #1 + Term 30   New Pmt _____   Red + Rate #2 + Term 40   New Pmt _____

Qualification Analysis: _____

Refi Pos ____ Yes ____ No Notes _____

Referral _____   Date _____

Short Sale Analysis:

Orig Value $_____   Orig Note $_____   Pres Value $_____   Pres Principal$_____

SP / Value _____

Prop Condition Notes: _____

Analysis Notes: _____

Figure 7:3 Sample Assessment Form – Page 3
This form is included for reference purposes only. You should obtain the applicable HUD or Lender forms for use in a negotiation.

Cause

The first questions you must ask the homeowner relates to the cause or reason behind the default. The nature of the financial hardship that has caused the default will point you to the first negotiation work out you should pursue. The type, severity, and term of the hardship will dictate the potential loss mitigation options that may apply to the file.

Example:	Item-Verifiable	Status	Potential Lowest Level Workout
	Job Loss	Temporary	Forbearance
	Divorce	Long-Term	Modification
	Death of a Party	Long-Term	Modification
	Injury	Variable	Further Research
	Disability	Long-Term	Modification
	Adjustable Rate	Currently Adjusting	Modification
	Family Addition	Long-Term	Modification
	Illness/Health Issue	Variable	Further Research

- Temporary issues may be viable candidates for a forbearance option, loan modification, legal assistance, employment aid, or credit counseling.

- Long-term issues may be able to resume financial responsibility with loan modification terms, but more likely will require more severe options such as a short sale or deed in lieu of foreclosure.

The ability to isolate the cause of the financial hardship is an essential skill in beginning the work out processes.

When making a determination regarding the cause of the financial hardship relating to an employment issue, you may complete a Verification of Employment (VOE) in addition to obtaining copies of the paycheck stub. The VOE is a form completed by the employer that provides details pertaining to the employment history, position, likelihood of continued employment, and any defined issues to continued employment. The contents of the paycheck stubs and VOE will assist in providing the lender with the third party verification of the homeowner's situation necessary to finalize a loss mitigation negotiation.

Verifications

If the default is the result of a loss in income, decrease in income, job loss or other employment related matter, referral to an applicable state employment-counseling center may assist the homeowner in regaining the financial ability to make the payments due under the note.

All loss mitigation negotiation will require verification of the statements given by the homeowner.

Example: Sudden job loss or temporary decrease in pay

Verification of status of employment

Example: Statement by the homeowner regarding a lack funds on hand (cash reserves) to meet the obligations of the mortgage or to perform necessary repairs at the property

Verification of Deposit

Verification proving the facts of the homeowners profile must be obtained from a third party who has access to specific details concerning factors relating to the situation of the homeowner.

It is important to understand a homeowner's right to financial privacy. Details concerning Financial Privacy and Authorization to Release/Obtain Information are included within the Ethics and Disclosure training.

The following pages provide you with example forms for specific situations.

- Verification of Employment (VOE)

- Verification of Deposit (VOD)

Each of these verification forms will provide specific information concerning your homeowner's situation, past, present and future.

You should forward these verification forms to the appropriate company or agency for completion. The forms should be accompanied by a copy of the homeowner's consent to release information.

REQUEST FOR VERIFICATION OF DEPOSIT

Privacy Act Notice: This information is to be used by the agency collecting it or its assignees in determining whether you qualify as a prospective mortgagor under its program. It will not be disclosed outside the agency except as required and permitted by law. You do not have to provide this information, but if you do not your application for approval as a prospective mortgagor or borrower may be delayed or rejected. The information requested in this form is authorized by Title 38, USC. Chapter 37 (if VA); by 12 USC, Section 1701 et. Seq (if HUD/FHA); by 42 USC, Section 1452b (if HUD/CPD); and Title 42 USC, 1471 et. Seq., or 7 USC. 1971 et. Deq. (if USDA/FmHA).

Instructions	Lender – Complete items 1 through 8. Have applicant complete item 9. Forward directly to depository named in item 1.
	Depository – Please complete Items 10 through 18 and return DIRECTLY to lender named in item 2.
	This form is to be transmitted directly to the lender and is not to be transmitted through the applicant or any other party.

PART I - REQUEST

1. To (Name and address of depository)	2. From (Name and address of Lender)

I certify that this verification has been sent directly to the bank or depository and ahs not passed through the hands of the applicant or any other interested party.

2. Signature of Lender	4. Title	4. Date	6. Lender's Number (Optional)

7. Information To Be Verified

Type of Account	Account in Name of	Account Number	Balance
			$
			$
			$

To Depository: I/We have applied for a mortgage loan and stated in my financial statement that the balance on deposit with you is as shown above. You are authorized to verify this information and to supply the lender identified above with the information requested in Items 10 through 13. Your response is solely a matter of courtesy for which no responsibility is attached to your institution or any of your officers.

8. Name and Address of Applicant(s)	9. Signature of Applicant(s)

PART II – VERIFICATION OF DEPOSITORY To Be Completed By Depository

10. Deposit Accounts of Applicant(s)

Type of Account	Account in Name of	Account Number	Balance
			$
			$
			$

11. Loans Outstanding To Applicants

Loan Number	Date of Loan	Original Amount	Current Balance	Installments (Monthly/Quarterly)		Secured By	Number of Late Payments
		$	$	$	per		
		$	$	$	per		
		$	$	$	per		

12. Please include any additional information which may be of assistance in determination of credit worthiness. (Please include information on loans paid-in-full in Item 11 above)

13. If the name(s) on the account(s) differ from those listed in Item 7, please supply the name(s) on the account(s) as reflected by your records.

PART III – Authorized Signature – Federal statutes provide severe penalty for any fraud, intentional misrepresentation, or criminal connivance or conspiracy purposed to influence the issuance of any guaranty or insurance by the VA Secretary, the U.S.D.A., FmHA/FHA Commissioner, or the HUD/CPD Assistant Secretary.

14. Signature of Depository Representative	15. Title (please print or type)	16. Date
17. Please print or type name signed in item 14	18. Phone No.	

Figure7:4 - Sample Form – VOD – HUD Release

REQUEST FOR VERIFICATION OF EMPLOYMENT

Privacy Act Notice: This information is to be used by the agency collecting it or its assignees in determining whether you qualify as a prospective mortgagor under its program. It will not be disclosed outside the agency except as required and permitted by law. You do not have to provide this information, but if you do not your application for approval as a prospective mortgagor or borrower may be delayed or rejected. The information requested in this form is authorized by Title 38, USC. Chapter 37 (if VA); by 12 USC, Section 1701 et. Seq (if HUD/FHA); by 42 USC, Section 1452b (if HUD/CPD); and Title 42 USC, 1471 et. Seq., or 7 USC. 1971 et. Deq. (if USDA/FmHA).

Instructions   Lender – Complete items 1 through 7. Have applicant complete item 8. Forward directly to employer named in item 1.
Employer – Please complete either Part II or Part III as applicable. Complete Part IV and return directly to lender named in item 2.
This form is to be transmitted directly to the lender and is not to be transmitted through the applicant or any other party.

Part I – Request

1. To (Name and address of employer)	2. From (Name and address of Lender)

I certify that this verification has been sent directly to the employer and ahs not passed through the hands of the applicant or any other interested party.

2. Signature of Lender	4. Title	4. Date	6. Lender's Number (Optional)

I have applied for a mortgage loan and stated that I am now or was formerly employed by you. My signature below authorizes verification of this information.

7. Name and Address of Applicant (include employee or badge number)	8. Signature of Applicant

Part II – Verification of Present Employment

9. Applicant's Date of Employment	10. Present Position	11. Probability of Continued Employment

12A. Current Gross Base Pay (enter Amount and Check Period)
__ Annual   __ Hourly
__ Monthly   __ Other (specify)
$ _____ __ Weekly

13 For Military Personnel Only

Pay Grade	
Type	Monthly Amount
Base Pay	$

14. If Overtime or Bonus is Applicable Is Its Continuance Likely?
Overtime   __ Yes __ No
Bonus   __ Yes __ No

15. If paid hourly – average hours per week

Type	Year to Date	Past Year 20_	Past Year 20_	Rations	$	
Base Pay	$	$	$	Flight or Hazard	$	16. Date of applicant's next pay increase
Overtime	$	$	$	Clothing	$	17. Projected amount of next pay increase
				Quarters	$	
Commissions	$	$	$	Pro Pay	$	18. Date of applicant's last pay increase
Bonus	$	$	$	Overseas or Combat	$	19. Amount of last pay increase
Total	$	$	$	Variable Housing Allowance	$	

20. Remarks (If employee was off work for any length of time, please indicate time period and reason)

Part III Verification of Previous Employment

21. Date Hired	23. Salary/Wage at Termination Per (Year) (Month) (Week)
22. Date Terminated	Base _____ Overtime _____ Commissions _____ Bonus _____
24. Reason for Leaving	25. Position Held

Part IV – Authorized Signature

Federal statutes provide severe penalties for any fraud, intentional misrepresentation, or criminal connivance or conspiracy purposed to influence the issuance of any guaranty or insurance by the VA Secretary, the U.S.D.A., FmHA/FHA Commissioner, or the HUD/CPD Assistant Secretary.

26. Signature of Employer	27. Title (please print or type)	28. Date
29. Print or type named signed in item 26	30. Phone No.	

Figure7:5 - Sample Form – VOE – HUD Release

Hardship Assessment

Income- Current/Future   The financial status of the homeowner will be reviewed.

Any homeowner who illustrates that they have the ability to pay the note but is still seeking loss mitigation negotiations may be disqualified.

These homeowners have the capacity to repay but have clearly chosen to use loss mitigation negotiations in an attempt to better their financial position.

While this may seem to be a sound financial strategy for the prudent homeowner, it is typically not of any benefit to the lender since the homeowner is CHOOSING not to make the payments on their mortgage in an attempt to better their position.

Lenders will usually negotiate only with those homeowners who can illustrate a financial need or hardship.

In order to determine both the current financial hardship and the ability of the homeowner to meet the debt obligations resulting from the negotiations, both present and future DTI calculations must be considered.

Debt-to-Income Ratio

The debt ratio is what will determine "how much" payment a homeowner can afford. The loss mitigation assessment will determine the DTI Ratio of the homeowner based on multiple situation contingencies.

Example: **Current ratio vs. affect of potential loan modification**

Minimum of two calculations

To make a determination regarding the appropriateness of a loan modification negotiation, you would determine

The DTI of the homeowner based on the current situation

The potential DTI if loan modifications are made to enable the resumption of payments

Example: **Current Ratio vs. Full Income Resumption**

Minimum of four calculations

To make a determination regarding the appropriateness of a temporary forbearance of the loan payments you would calculate

The DTI of the homeowner based on the current situation

The potential DTI of the homeowner when the temporary income reduction matter is resolved and regular mortgage payments are resumed

The surplus income available to the homeowner during the forbearance may enable the maintenance of a partial payment.

The surplus income of the homeowner when the temporary income reduction matter is resolved and regular mortgage payments are resumed. The surplus income analysis will assist in determining the post-forbearance repayment plan.

When calculating the Pre-Modification DTI Ratio you will complete the questionnaire, determine what calculations may be applicable to the transaction, and then complete those calculations to assess the level of the hardship. The level of the hardship must be equal to or greater then the minimum requirements of the lender. The lender will often deny a negotiations attempt for a homeowner whose financial hardship falls within a minimum category. The level of hardship will be defined by the DTI Ratio limitations set by the lender.

The hardship assessment will also provide details relating to the potential loss mitigation options that are available for the homeowner. The goal of the loss mitigation retention options is to stabilize the ability of the homeowner to regain financial stability and resume normal payments.

Sample Standard guidelines   The ratio of mortgage payment to income be equal to or less than 29% AND / OR

The ratio of ALL debt including mortgage payment, taxes, insurance, and all other regular revolving or fixed loan expense of the homeowner be equal to or less 41%

Typical debts used to determine the qualifying ratios:

- the house payment
- the minimum required monthly payments on all of the following:

    Auto Loans

    Student Loans

    Personal Loans

    Charge Cards   minimum required payments only (all open credit accounts will be counted at the minimum payment even if there is no balance outstanding. The availability of the credit line requires a payment to be factored.)

    Child Support

    Alimony

    Federal Tax Lien Repayment Schedules

    State Tax Lien Repayment Schedules

    Other open debt may be a consideration if it is an open line, with regular monthly payments and is not a part of housing or personal maintenance.

Typical monthly liabilities that you will **NOT** use to calculate debt ratios:

    Utility Bills

    Car & Health Insurance

    Cell Phone Bills

This is not to be considered an all-inclusive list. The lists included for review are for example purposes only. Other debt may exist in the homeowner profile.

The percentage of all debt to income is often termed the back-end ratio.

The percentage of only mortgage debt to income is often termed the front-end ratio

You will use specific financial data when completing the base DTI calculation

Income	= $3,000
Mortgage Payment	= $ 900
Minimum Monthly Payments	= $ 300

CALCULATION

Mortgage	+	Monthly Payments	=	Debt Load
900	+	300	=	1200

Debt Load	/	Income	=	40%
1200	/	3000	=	40%

In this scenario,

The front-end (mortgage payment only) is 30%.

30% is a questionable debt load under many guidelines.

The back-end (all applicable debt) is 40%

40% is considered an acceptable debt load under many guidelines.

This homeowner would need to illustrate another reason why they are unable to meet the current mortgage obligations before most lenders would consider entering loss mitigation negotiations.

Example: Major family medical issue creating excess medical expense

Medical expense is typically not factored as part of the DTI Ratio but might cause a temporary financial hardship.

The homeowner might obtain temporary relief until the medical matter is resolved through a forbearance arrangement with the lender.

To determine the applicability of the forbearance, you would need to gather documentation

- proving the medical emergency and expense

- defining the likely duration of medical emergency

- illustrating the inability to meet the medical emergency needs and the mortgage debt requirements

- proving the homeowner's ability to begin resuming stipulated loan payment PLUS an additional payment to offset the arrearages

Debt-to-Income practice exercises are included within the skill building CD component of your coursework. It is important that you become adept at the calculation of debt to income ratios. The DTI will play a large role the loss mitigation negotiation process.

DEBT TO INCOME RATIO (DTI%)

Monthly Income

Homeowner

$_____ Base Pay/ _____

$_____ Commission/ _____

$_____ Other _____

$_____ Other _____

$_____ Total Monthly Income

Co-Homeowner

$_____ Base Pay/ _____

$_____ Commission/ _____

$_____ Other _____

$_____ Other _____

$_____ Total Monthly Income

Combined Current Monthly Income $_____

Income Notes: _____

Define any income adjustments that apply, the reason for these adjustments, and the duration of the applicable adjustment. Provide date of income change.

Adjusted Monthly Income: Date of Adjustment: _____ Reason: _____

Homeowner

$_____ Base Pay/ _____

$_____ Commission/ _____

$_____ Other _____

$_____ Other _____

$_____ Total Expected Monthly Income

Co-Homeowner

$_____ Base Pay/ _____

$_____ Commission/ _____

$_____ Other _____

$_____ Other _____

$_____ Total Expected Monthly Income

Combined Adjusted Monthly Income $_____

Figure7:6 - Sample Form – DTI – Page 1

Current Monthly Debt

Homeowner	Co-Homeowner
$_____ House/Rent Payment	$_____ House/Rent Payment(factor once)
$_____ Automobile Payment	$_____ Automobile Payment
$_____ Credit Card _____	$_____ Credit Card _____
$_____ Credit Card _____	$_____ Credit Card _____
$_____ Credit Card _____	$_____ Credit Card _____
$_____ Personal Loan _____	$_____ Personal Loan _____
$_____ Other_____	$_____ Other_____
$_____ Other_____	$_____ Other_____
$_____ Total Monthly Debt	$_____ Total Monthly Debt

Combined Current Monthly Debt $_____

Debt Notes: _____

Define any debt adjustments that apply, the reason for these adjustments, and the duration of the applicable adjustment. Provide date of debt change.

Adjusted Monthly Debt: Date of Adjustment: _____   Reason: _____

Adjusted Monthly Debt

Homeowner	Co-Homeowner
$_____ House/Rent Payment	$_____ House/Rent Payment(factor once)
$_____ Automobile Payment	$_____ Automobile Payment
$_____ Credit Card _____	$_____ Credit Card _____
$_____ Credit Card _____	$_____ Credit Card _____
$_____ Credit Card _____	$_____ Credit Card _____
$_____ Personal Loan _____	$_____ Personal Loan _____
$_____ Other_____	$_____ Other_____
$_____ Other_____	$_____ Other_____
$_____ Total Monthly Debt	$_____ Total Monthly Debt

Combined Adjusted Monthly Debt $_____

Figure7:7 - Sample Form – DTI – Page 2

Forbearance Calculations

Current DTI Calculations

Take the total debt $_____ (factor each debt only once – if it is a joint debt list under the primary income earner only) and divide by the current combined income $_____ the total is the current DTI.

Debt _____ / Current Income _____ = Current DTI _____%

Future Calculations

Take the total debt $_____ and divide by the Future / Expected combined income $_____ the total is the expected DTI.

Debt _____ / Future Income _____ = Expected DTI _____%

Modification Calculation

Current Calculations

Add all liabilities EXCEPT mortgage _____ divide by the combined monthly income _____ the total is the other liability DTI of the homeowner.

Take the current mortgage debt $_____ and divide by the combined monthly income _____ the total is the Front End DTI.

Current Mortgage Debt _____ / Combined Income _____ = Front End DTI _____%

Mortgage (Front End DTI)% _____ + All other Debt DTI %_____ = Back End DTI _____%

Post Modification Calculations

Add all liabilities EXCEPT mortgage _____ divide by the combined monthly income _____ the total is the other liability DTI of the homeowner.

Take the current mortgage debt $_____ and divide by the combined monthly income _____ the total is the Front End DTI.

Current Mortgage Debt _____ / Combined Income _____ = Front End DTI _____ %

Mortgage (Front End DTI)% _____ + All other Debt DTI %_____ = Back End DTI _____ %

SURPLUS INCOME

Many lenders will want to know the surplus income available to the homeowner both before and after any loss mitigation action.

This surplus income before the loss mitigation action will effect the lender's negotiation decisions in any refinance, short sale, deed in lieu of foreclosure and reinstatement negotiations.

The surplus income calculations after the implementation of loss mitigation options will be used by the lender in any negotiation for forbearance and loan modification negotiation.

Calculating the 'surplus income' ratio is a continuance of the basic DTI Ratio calculation. You will factor the current and future DTI ratio regardless of the variances in the application of negotiation points.

Example: Temporary income reduction calculation

Post loan modification calculation

1.   Total all normal monthly living expenses including the mortgage applicable for the estimate over the period being calculated

Example: Forbearance
Current Mortgage + Estimated Debt
(forbearance period)

2.   Total all anticipated income for the period being calculated

3.   Subtract the estimated expense from the estimated income to determine surplus income during the applicable period.

You will complete these calculations in the same manner to determine the surplus income of each potential situation.

Example: Post Forbearance Calculation

    Anticipated Post-Forbearance Income
-   Anticipated Post-Forbearance Debt Load

=   Post-Forbearance Surplus Income

The post-forbearance surplus income can be used to assess the ability of the homeowner to make additional payments toward the payment of the arrearages created by the pre-forbearance default and payments delayed during the forbearance.

Credit Report

Every action a consumer takes affects their credit report. These actions can have a negative or a positive effect.

Credit reports are an overview of a person's entire history of spending and payment habits. Almost everything that a person does financially is collected, reported, and stored in the credit profile. The primary concern of a loss mitigation specialist is the reporting of debt load, liens that may affect the subject property, and the status of other debt that may make a refinance transaction a potential loss mitigation option.

Credit Terminology

Debt: is the term describing any situation in which funds are borrowed.

Debt Load: is the amount of debt an individual is carrying (owes).

                             Debt load may include many items. The most common being:

                                 Credit card debt

                                 Department store debt

Charge accounts

Auto loans

Student loans

Mortgages

The ability to borrow more money or to have additional credit extended is affected by how much debt a potential homeowner currently carries.

As a loss mitigation specialist, you will factor many different applications of the debt ratio including, current ratio, expected ratio after crises remedy, modification ratio, and surplus income ratio.

Debt-to-Income Ratio's are the amount of open debt a homeowner has available weighed against the homeowner's monthly income.

The higher the DTI the greater the potential risk of a homeowner default on the loan.

The credit report will provide a relatively accurate view of current debt load. The homeowner will provide income documentation, verification of hardship, and other income related items to enable comparison of current and expected financial status against loss mitigation option guidelines.

Late payments include any payment that has been made more than 30 days past the due date

Late payments can be a severe blemish on the credit report.

Mortgage late payments will be included on the report as part of the default. If you receive a consumer loss mitigation assessment request before late payments begin, you may have a case for referral to a refinance lender. The ability of a traditional lender to provide a refinance for the homeowner will be based on

Acceptable Debt to Income Ratio

Acceptable Property Value

Acceptable Credit History

Acceptable Employment History

Example of early inquiry:

- A homeowner has an adjustable rate mortgage

- The first rate adjustment has occurred recently or is about to occur

- The homeowner has been able to maintain payment on all obligations so there are not late payment entries

- The homeowner will be unable to maintain these timely payments with the new mortgage amount due as a result of the adjustable rate

- If the homeowner has a reasonable credit history, employment history and loan to value ratio, the homeowner may qualify for a traditional refinance

You should gain an understanding of how to rate the late payments present on the credit report. If a homeowner may qualify for a refinance transaction, you should refer the file to a loan officer within your bank or to a reputable lender in your area if you are functioning as an external loss mitigation specialist.

Refinance lenders are typically reviewing the previous two-year payment history.

A late payment will appear on the credit report for two years, though credit bureaus may keep them in the credit file for up to seven years.

Bankruptcy actions can remain on the credit report for as long as 10 years.

An active bankruptcy is a significant factor the loss mitigation specialist must consider when reviewing a homeowner assessment.

If the homeowner has entered bankruptcy, the loss mitigation efforts may be halted during the bankruptcy process.

If the loss mitigation file you are assessing contains an open, active bankruptcy, you should refer the case to a supervisor if you are acting on behalf of the lender or contact the homeowner's attorney if you are acting at the direction of the homeowner. The details of loss mitigation during bankruptcy are numerous and may vary by the applicable statutes of the homeowner.

Collection accounts are accounts that a homeowner fails to pay as agreed.

These accounts are turned over to a collection department within the structure of the original creditor, a collection agency or another service in the attempt to collect the payments owed. The initial creditor and the collection agencies report these accounts to the bureaus.

> Collection accounts may be in repayment. Any repayment agreement will be included in the debt to income calculations you will complete on the file.
>
> Collection accounts may also be effect the lien condition of the title to the property.

It is important that you assess the status of any collection accounts and determine how these accounts may affect the loss mitigation calculations and negotiation position of the parties.

Credit Bureau Scores: are the scores generated based solely on the data contained within the credit report. A Fair, Isaac Credit Bureau Score, is sometimes referred to as a FICO score. The FICO Score is calculated using a system of scorecards.

Credit scoring has been around since the 1950's and Credit Bureau Scores became widely available in the 1980's.

Credit Scores are now used extensively in such industries as mortgage lending, auto lending, and bankcards.

Most loss mitigation options do not include an assessment of the homeowner's credit score. If the file has the potential for referral to a refinance lender, the score may become a factor.

Credit Bureau scoring is a scientific way of assessing how likely a homeowner is to pay back a loan.

How is the CBS calculated?

A Credit Bureau Score is based on the data available in the homeowner's credit report.

The score measures the relative degree of risk a potential homeowner represents to the lender or investor.

A credit bureau score is not a measure of a homeowner's income, assets, or bank account. These factors are calculated and assessed independent of credit scores.

In developing the credit scorecards, Fair, Isaac uses actual credit data from millions of consumers. They apply complex mathematical methods and perform extensive research into credit patterns that enable them to forecast credit performance.

Through this process, the repository identifies distinctive credit patterns. Each pattern corresponds to a likelihood that a consumer will make his or her loan payments as agreed.

This score is based on all of the credit-related data in the credit bureau report, not just negative data such as a missed mortgage payment or a bankruptcy.

The score will consider the amount of credit a borrower has available, the amount of credit the borrower is using compared to these limits, the types of credit a borrower has available, and the borrowers payment performance on their credit obligations among other factors.

Score Range: The approximate range of the Fair, Isaac Credit Bureau Scores range is between 450 to 850 points.

Repositories: Credit scores are available through three national repositories.

The scoring programs of these credit bureaus are called:

BEACON   at EQUIFAX (CBI)

EMPIRICA   at TRANS UNION

TRW/FAIR, ISAAC   at TRW

This score is calculated at the repository and is based on the data within that repositories credit file.

Score Data: The types of credit information used in the credit bureau scorecards are typically the same items underwriter will use to make a credit decision. These can include:

Payment history

Public records and collection items

Severity, recentness, and frequency of delinquencies noted in the trade line section

Outstanding Debt

Number of balances recently reported

Average balance across all trade lines

Relationship between total balances and total credit limits on revolving trade lines

Credit History

Age of oldest trade line

Inquiries and new account openings

Number of inquiries in the last year

Number of new accounts opened in the last year

Amount of time since most recent inquiry

Types of credit in use

Number of trade lines for each type:

> Bankcard
> Travel and Entertainment cards
> Department store cards
> Personal finance company references
> Installment loans
> Other credit

Fair, Isaac observes tens of thousands of credit report histories of mortgage homeowners to determine which credit report items or combination of items are the most predictive of future risk. This data indicates the amount of weight each item should contribute to a credit decision.

FAIR, ISAAC CREDIT BUREAU SCORES DO NOT USE RACE, COLOR, RELIGION, NATIONAL ORIGIN, SEX,

MARITAL STATUS, OR AGE AS PREDICTIVE CHARACTERISTICS.

OCCUPATION AND LENGTH OF TIME IN PRESENT HOUSING ARE ALSO NOT USED IN THE SCORECARDS.

ANY INFORMATION THAT IS NOT PRESENT IN THE CREDIT FILE IS NOT USED IN CREATING A CREDIT BUREAU SCORECARD.

Understanding a score's impact

The credit report will contain one or multiple credit scores followed by a series of score factor reason codes. This numerical score is often termed a fair isaac credit bureau score and it is a means of rank ordering potential borrowers based on the likelihood that they will pay their credit obligations as agreed.

A higher score indicates a better credit quality. If all other things in the borrower profile were equal, a borrower with a credit score of 642 is more likely to pay their debts as agreed than a borrower with a score of 537.

The Fair, Isaac Credit Bureau Score is a means of rank-ordering potential homeowners based on the likelihood that they will pay their credit obligations as agreed.

A higher score indicates a better credit quality. If all other things are equal, homeowners with a score of 640 are less likely to default on a loan then homeowners with a score of 560.

The Fair Isaac Credit Bureau Score models at each credit repository are of similar design. The scores are scaled to indicate a similar level of risk across all three repositories. In other words, a score of 660 at one bureau will represent a similar level of risk as a score of 660 at another bureau.

The risk is defined in terms of the number of accounts that remain in good standing compared to those that default.

Sample credit score ranges for new mortgage borrowers from a national sample	
Score Range	Number of good loans for each bad loan showing delinquency or foreclosure (# of good to 1 bad)
Below 600	8 to 1
700 – 719	123 to 1
Above 800	1,292 to 1

Credit Bureau Scores will rank-order potential borrowers based on risk or the number of good loans to bad loans denoted by a score. This rank ordering is likely to fluctuate due to changes in the economy, regional differences, changes in product offerings, or other reasons.

A lender who uses scores for rank order potential borrower is basing their guideline tiers of risk on historical data related to the files that they have processed and closed in the past. The levels or approval tier that the lender uses is likely to fluctuate over time due to changes in the economy. The lender will create approval tiers and loan product offerings by comparing the performance of their loans over time. This enables them to determine the relationship of borrower performance by market environment, credit score, and other details.

Report Appearance

Credit reports can take multiple visual forms depending on the bureau that issued the report and the type of record being requested. Regardless of the initial visual variations, all credit reports contain the same basic elements. These include borrower details and data, a summary of all of the credit inclusions, and a detailed breakdown of the borrower's current and historical credit transactions. Each section of the report will contain details that will assist you in determining if the potential borrower will qualify for one of your loan programs.

The upper portion of credit report will typically include identifying information including your name or company name as the individual, who requested the report.

Report type will usually be included in the header. Report type may be individual or joint.

Information relating to the individual within the credit bureau who pulled the report and the internal case ID # assigned to the report will be defined in the header of the report. This information will be important if you must request updates to the report or address a discrepancy in the report with the credit bureau.

MERGED INFILE CREDIT REPORT

Prepared For:	Property Address:	Prepared By:	Date Rec:
Attention:	Loan Type: Purpose of Loan: Report Type:	Computer ID: Lender Case #:	Date Comp: Date Revised:

APPLICANT

Name:			
SSN:	DOB:		
Marital Status:	Dependents:		
:			
Home Phone:			
Present Address:			
Since:	Own / Rent		
Previous Address:			
From:	To:	Own / Rent	

CO-APPLICANT

Name:			
SSN:	DOB:		
Marital Status:	Dependents:		
:			
Home Phone:			
Present Address:			
Since:	Own / Rent		
Previous Address:			
From:	To:	Own / Rent	

Date data will be included within the report. Date data can include the date the request was received by the credit bureau, the date the credit bureau completed the report, and the date of any revisions created by the credit bureau in relationship to the report.

Date is important because underwriting typically stipulates that the report must be current, or within a certain date range, in order to be used for closing.

Foreclosure Prevention – Loss Mitigation Specialist

Homeowner Information

The credit report will contain details relating to the individual or individuals to whom the credit report applies.

This portion includes specifics such as full name, social security number, and date of birth. Information relating to the homeowner's address and employment may be included in this segment of the report. It is important that you remember that information you have gained directly from the homeowner may be more up-to-date than information contained within the credit report.

Variations in homeowner address and employment are common within the report. You should note any discrepancy between the report and your file information and verify with the homeowner to ensure that the report does not contain entries that relate to another individual with a similar name. If you note a discrepancy, you must address these differences before the package is submitted to underwriting.

MERGED INFILE CREDIT REPORT

Prepared For:	Property Address:	Prepared By:	Date Rec:
Attention:	Loan Type: Purpose of Loan: Report Type:	Computer ID: Lender Case #:	Date Comp: Date Revised:

APPLICANT / CO-APPLICANT

APPLICANT		CO-APPLICANT	
Name: SSN: Marital Status: Home Phone:	DOB: Dependents:	Name: SSN: Marital Status: Home Phone:	DOB: Dependents:
Present Address:		Present Address:	
Since:	Own / Rent	Since:	Own / Rent
Previous Address:		Previous Address:	
From: To:	Own / Rent	From: To:	Own / Rent

Borrower and Co-Borrower identifying information is entered in this section.

You should verify that all details entered match the information included on the loss mitigation summary.

Credit Summary

The credit report will contain a segment that summarizes the details contained within the actual report. You should review this area to ensure that the inclusions do not bring to mind a red flag issue. You may need to question the homeowner more closely regarding these matters.

CREDIT SUMMARY

	PAYMENTS	BALANCES	LIMITS	TRADES	30+	60+	90+
REVOLVING	0	2061	2200	4	4	4	17
INSTALLMENT 1307	1307	79365	90610	25	34	8	27
REAL ESTATE	378	35384	36600	1	2	0	0
OPEN/OTHER	991	1041	1041	5	0	0	0
TOTAL	2676	117851	129451	38	40	12	44

# INQUIRIES	50	# PUBLIC RECORDS	0	# BANKRUPTCIES	0
WORST TRADE	9	OLDEST DATE	07/01/89	# SATISFACTORIES	17

The summary will contain details identifying the types of credit that the borrower has available. You wish to ensure that the types and amount of credit available to the homeowner is exported into the DTI Analysis Form.

If you are using a system that does not automatically export report data into the Analysis Forms, you will need to enter each credit account, payment, and status by hand.

Credit payment totals and current balances will appear within the credit summary portion of your report.

You will confirm the payment information when you review the report inclusions.

Then you will use this information to confirm the debt ratio information and begin isolating potential loss mitigation options for the homeowner.

A summary data analysis of the details of the report will be included within the summary. This analysis will assist you in completing the scoring key. Much of the data you will use during credit scoring and mitigation screening will be summarized with in this section. Before you export the data into the credit-scoring key, debt-to-income ratio form, or loss mitigation application, you must review the report with the homeowner to ensure that all of the inclusions of the summary are correct and relate to active accounts. You will confirm the status of each account by reviewing the detail pages of the credit report.

CREDIT SUMMARY

	PAYMENTS	BALANCES	LIMITS	TRADES	30+	60+	90+
REVOLVING	0	2061	2200	4	4	4	17
INSTALLMENT 1307	1307	79365	90610	25	34	8	27
REAL ESTATE	378	35384	36600	1	2	0	0
OPEN/OTHER	991	1041	1041	5	0	0	0
TOTAL	2676	117851	129451	38	40	12	44

INQUIRIES   50   # PUBLIC RECORDS   0   # BANKRUPTCIES   0
WORST TRADE 9   OLDEST DATE   07/01/89   # SATISFACTORIES   17

The number of inquiries into credit profile will be totaled and entered into the summary.

A detailed breakdown of the companies that made credit inquiries will be included at the end of the report.

The homeowner may be required to provide an explanation for any excessive inquiries.

Credit inquiries may indicate that the homeowner has already attempted to remedy the delinquency through outside measures, such as a refinance.

You should review the data relating to these inquiries and discuss the results of any outside efforts the homeowner has made.

Specifics regarding public records, bankruptcy, and the worst trade payment history that you will encounter in the report will be included within the credit summary.

You should note these entries to ensure that you locate the applicable data within the report relating to any bankruptcy, late payment, or public record detailed within the summary.

Public records could relate to liens placed against the property not related to a mortgage or refinance. These liens could become a factor in loss mitigation negotiations where the surrender of the property is being considered.

If a judgment or public record exists in the borrower profile, the details of that record will be included within the report.

This data could include bankruptcy or foreclosure actions as well as judgments and other public records.

CREDIT SUMMARY

	PAYMENTS	BALANCES	LIMITS	TRADES	30+	60+	90+
REVOLVING	0	2061	2200	4	4	4	17
INSTALLMENT 1307	1307	79365	90610	25	34	8	27
REAL ESTATE	378	35384	36600	1	2	0	0
OPEN/OTHER	991	1041	1041	5	0	0	0
TOTAL	2676	117851	129451	38	40	12	44

# INQUIRIES	50	# PUBLIC RECORDS	0	# BANKRUPTCIES	0
WORST TRADE	9	OLDEST DATE	07/01/89	# SATISFACTORIES	17

The oldest date field indicates the date that the borrower fist obtained credit.

This inclusion allows you to ensure that an adequate credit history is available to the borrower. Many underwriting guidelines will require the potential borrower have at least a two-year credit history with at least three open active trade lines. If your potential borrower does not have a sufficient credit history or quantity of accounts, you may need to take alternative actions to aid the borrower in creating a credit profile that meets the minimum requirements of the loan guidelines.

It is important to address any issues early in the prequalification process. Proactively addressing issues early in the process helps to minimize stipulation requests, speeds the loan process, and facilitates positive relationships with borrowers, referral partners, and affinity service providers. This positive relationship building activity helps to ensure that your office gains the reputation as the office that can get the job done.

If a judgment or public record exists in the borrower profile, the details of that record will be included within the report.

This data could include bankruptcy or foreclosure actions as well as judgments and other public records.

You should scrutinize any inclusion within this section thoroughly to determine the status of the public record, the age of the public record, and the manner that the record will affect your borrower's approval status.

The type of public record will be named.

This typing will indicate to you the specific handling of the matter per the loss mitigation option that is being considered for the homeowner.

The report will include the dates pertaining to the specific public record.

The opened date will indicate the age of the judgment.

The last active date may affect the handling of the record depending upon the specific loss mitigation option being considered for the homeowner.

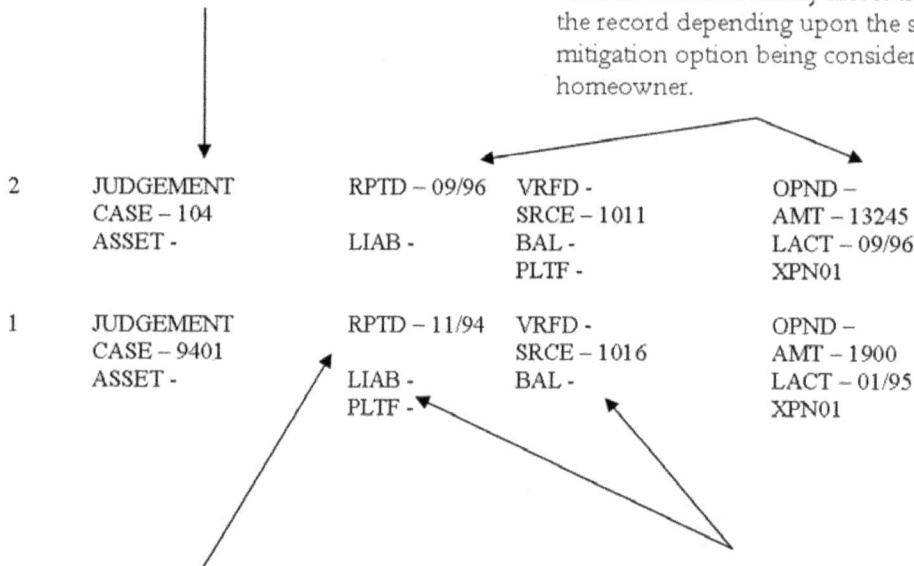

| 2 | JUDGEMENT CASE – 104 ASSET - | RPTD – 09/96 LIAB - | VRFD - SRCE – 1011 BAL - PLTF - | OPND – AMT – 13245 LACT – 09/96 XPN01 |
| 1 | JUDGEMENT CASE – 9401 ASSET - | RPTD – 11/94 LIAB - PLTF - | VRFD - SRCE – 1016 BAL - | OPND – AMT – 1900 LACT – 01/95 XPN01 |

Data regarding the status of the record will be included.

A satisfied judgment or closed bankruptcy will affect your file differently than an open or active record.

The liability or balance of the record will be included.

You will want to verify these figures and compare them to the specific
Loss Mitigation option being considered for the homeowner.

Loss Mitigation handling of liens against the property will vary.

Example: Forbearance – liens may not be an issue in the negotiation of forbearance unless they dictate a higher DTI Ratio that makes the maintenance of future mortgage payments unlikely

Short Sale – all outstanding liens against the property, including those held by judgment must be discharged or paid in full in order to provide the marketable title that will be necessary at the time the property is transferred.

Score Factors

The name of the repository issuing the credit score included with the report will be included.

The code of the applicable agency will be entered to confirm the source of the score.

EFX = Equifax

The lender negotiating the loss mitigation workout will designate the repository score that will be used for the process.

This designation is a result of regional

| 8 | BEACON SCORE | EFX01 |

519
SERIOUS DELINQUENCY AND DEROGATORY PUBLIC RECORD OR COLLECTION FILED
AMOUNT OWED ON DELINQUENT ACCOUNTS
PROPORTION OF BALANCES TO CREDIT LIMITS TOO HIGH ON REVOLVING ACCOUNTS
LENGTH OF TIME ACCOUNTS HAVE BEEN ESTABLISHED

| 8 | EMPIRICA SCORE | TRU01 |

493
SERIOUS DELINQUENCY, AND PUBLIC RECORD OR COLLECTION FILED
LEVEL OF DELINQUENCY ON ACCOUNTS
TIME SINCE DELINQUENCY IS TOO RECENT OR UNKNOWN
PROPORTION OF REVOLVING BALANCES TO REVOLVING CREDIT LIMITS IS TOO HIGH

| 8 | FAIR ISAAC SCORE | XPN01 |

529
SERIOUS DELINQUENCY AND PUBLIC RECORD OR COLLECTION FILED
PROPORTION OF BALANCES TOO HIGH ON REVOLVING ACCOUNTS
NUMBER OF ACCOUNTS DELINQUENT
LENGTH OF TIME SINCE LEGAL ITEM FILED OR COLLECTION ITEM REPORTED

The factors that affect the score will be included on the report. This information is often referred to by a score factor code.

Score Factors – Reason Codes

To understand why a credit report scored the way it did, you must review the reason codes given within each score. These reason codes provide the top reasons why a profile did not score higher. These codes only indicate the top reasons and other factors probably contribute to the overall score. You should review both the score and the reasons the score ranks where it does with your customer.

To find the scores you should locate a number or a letter followed by a brief description.

For example, a score of 540 may have the following factors

- 02 – Delinquency on accounts

- 01 – Amount owed on accounts is too high

- 09 – Too many accounts opened in the last 12 months

- 19 – Too few accounts currently paid as agreed

Score factors are less meaningful for higher scoring credit records as they merely point to the reasons why a very good credit report was not perfect.

Examples of adverse factors that may appear on the report as a consideration in the score calculation are

- Current outstanding balances on accounts
- Delinquency report on accounts
- Accounts not paid as agreed
- Too few open accounts
- Too many open accounts
- Too many bank accounts with outstanding balances
- Too many finance company accounts
- Payment history too new to rate
- Number of inquiries within the last 12 months
- Number of accounts opened within the last 12 months
- Balance too high
- Length of credit history
- No recent account information
- Too few accounts rate as current
- Amount past due on accounts
- No adverse factors
- Recent derogatory public record or collection

This is not an all-inclusive listing. The items listed are examples of issues you may find in the score coding section of a report. You should review each report carefully to determine the factors specific to that credit profile.

FRAUD ALERT

The fraud alert field is becoming increasingly filled field within today's environment. Any data that indicates possible fraud activity will be included with in this section. The information will often become a warning entry because of some action taken by the borrower but any entry other than "available and clear" should be reviewed and discussed with the homeowner.

Basic information noted by the credit bureau as potential fraud will be flagged.

If the entry is not related to an action taken by the homeowner, the homeowner may be a victim of identity theft and all entries in the body of the report should be scrutinized to ensure that all of the accounts do belong to the borrower.

An example of a fraud alert entry would be the number of inquiries in the last 60 days.

Excessive inquiries may be a result of attempts on the part of the homeowner to seek a solution to the mortgage default process. In this case, there is little cause for concern as the alert is related to an action taken by your homeowner.

FRAUD ALERT

1	TRANS ALERT # INQUIRIES IN LAST 60 DAYS: 04 RECORDED INQUIRIES ALTER	TRU01
1	HAWK ALERT HAWK AVAILABLE AND CLEAR	TRU 01

Details regarding any activity that may indicate fraud will be included.

AVAILABLE AND CLEAR = No information found

inquiries in the last 60 days = potential credit gathering spree.

At times, this could indicate a stolen profile but more often, this insert is related to the search current loan search.

CREDIT HISTORY DETAILS

The main body of the report will contain details of each account contained within the homeowner's credit history. You will wish to scrutinize each entry within this section to determine the status of the homeowner's credit, gain an understanding of the homeowner's payment and spending habits, and complete the credit history-scoring key.

The credit history-scoring key will be explained later and is included within the appendix section of your workbook. This key will assist you in extracting the necessary details from the credit profile.

CREDIT HISTORY

E C O A	CREDITOR ACCOUNT NO	DATE RPTED	DATE LAST ACT	DATE OPND	LIMIT / HIGHEST CREDIT	PRESENT STATUS		TERMS	PAY AMT	TYPE AND ACCT STATUS	HISTORICAL STATUS			
						BALANCE OWING	AMOUNT PAST DUE				NO MOS HIIST REV	3 0	60	9 0
8	AFM-BLOOM #APRINTLO COLLECTION	02/99	04/94		425	425				OPN05				

The name of the creditor and the account number will be included within the report.

Account numbers are often shortened on the credit report and the full account number may not appear. You can obtain the full account number directly from your homeowner if it is a necessary element of the loss mitigation process.

For example, a refinance transaction may require certain bills to be paid in full as part of the transaction. You will need to obtain the full account number for each account to confirm the pay off amount and to ensure that all payments are allocated correctly at the closing.

CREDIT HISTORY

E C O A	CREDITOR ACCOUNT NO	DATE RPTED	DATE LAST ACT	DATE OPND	LIMIT / HIGHEST CREDIT	PRESENT STATUS								
						BALANCE OWING	AMOUNT PAST DUE							
8	AFM-BLOOM #APRINTLO COLLEC-TION	02/99	04/94		425	425								

The date reported is the last reporting date for a particular account.

Not all creditors report on a monthly basis.

You may be required to bring the data pertaining to a specific account up to date to comply with specific underwriting requirements and to ensure that no derogatory data exists for the last months of the account.

The date last active provides you with information relating to the last date the account was in use.

Some accounts will be closed and will not effect of the transaction.

You should review the last active date before including the account in your history score.

The opening date of the account allows you to review the historical status with more accuracy.

The date opened may also help you to define when the homeowner began to have financial issues. This information is helpful when proving that the loss mitigation need is a result of a specific financial hardship and not an indication of poor planning or credit use on the part of the homeowner.

The present status details the current balances and any amounts currently due or past due for each account.

You should scan this column to note any issues that may arise during qualification and workout processes.

Past due accounts may lead to a lien against the subject property and should be considered during the workout planning.

The terms field shows you the original and the current agreement relating to the payments and terms of the account.

A revolving account or credit card will typically not provide you with an end date for the payments as these amounts will fluctuate depending on the borrower's spending actions.

If the account is an installment note, the column will give you the payment terms agreed upon for the account.

Payment amount will provide you with the minimum payment that is due on the account.

You will export these payment amounts into the debt-to-income ratio calculation form.

If the account has no payment entered, it may be an inactive account or it may be a revolving account that does not currently have a balance.

Even if an account does not have a balance, if credit is available to the borrower you must factor a minimum payment into the debt ratio for that account.

The underwriting guidelines will define the payment amount you will use.

CREDIT HISTORY

ECOA	CREDITOR ACCOUNT NO	DATE RPTED	DATE LAST ACT	DATE OPND	LIMIT / HIGHEST CREDIT	PRESENT STATUS		TERMS	PAY AMT	TYPE AND ACCT STATUS	HISTORICAL STATUS			
						BALANCE OWING	AMOUNT PAST DUE				NO MOS HIIST REV	30	60	90
8	AFM-BLOOM #APRINTLO COLLECTION	02/99	04/94		425	425				OPN05				

HISTORICAL STATUS details allow you to review the credit history as well as determine if a specific credit issues exists in relationship to a particular account.

NO MOS HIST REV indicates the number of months detailed within the historical data section.

The numerical entries indicate the status of the payments to be found within the report.

Each account history will contain numbers indicating the status of a particular month's payment.

1 = on time
2 = 30 days late
3 = 60 days late
X = same as previous month

Read the history from LEFT to RIGHT.

Type and account status will provide you with the type of account and its present status.

- Revolving   REV
- Installment   Ins
- Mortgage   Mtg
- Consumer   Cons

This field could also contain derogatory accounts such as collections, charge offs or judgments.

- The number of month's history shows the numbers of months reported on the history of the account.

  The type of hardship the homeowner is stating and the specific lender guidelines will dictate the number of months that must be reviewed for each account.

- When you review the account, you will be seeking the status of the account.

  In other words, you will review the account to determine whether the payments were made on time or if any late payment exists within the history.

- You will also look for the date of each payment reference.

- The historical status and late payments section provides you with numerical entries that indicate any late payments that will be found within the report.

  Each account history will contain numbers indicating the status of a particular month's payment.

  1 = on time

  2 = 30 days late

  3 = 60 days late

  X = the same status as the previous month

This section of the history summary will provide you with the number of times a borrower has been on time, 30 days, and 60 days late during the reported credit history.

An account shows a 1 indicates that the account was paid on time within the history.

➢ When you note an account that contains derogatory information or a credit blemish, you should first confirm that the account is active and that the derogatory account is recent and the entry applies to the process.

➢ You will then determine the last date that the account is reported and begin counting backwards from the last entry.

You will review account details by moving from left to right.

Example: The reporting of this account begins in July.

The first entry is July. Moving backwards from Left to Right the next entries are

June	=	On Time
May	=	30 Days Late
April	=	On Time

and then backwards through time all of the payments were made on time.

Example: The next account was reported in June so the backwards counting will begin with the month of June.

You will need to obtain an update for this account that illustrates the payment in July to bring this account current with the other entries on the report.

When you locate an account that illustrates a late payment, you will enter a 1x30 day late into the status section of your credit history-scoring key.

You will complete this process for every account in the report that contains a derogatory entry. You will export any credit blemish or derogatory entry you find on the credit report into your credit history.

Many people find it helpful to note any derogatory or important data directly on the report prior to exporting this information onto the credit history-scoring key. This helps to ensure that you do not skip any important factors during the export processes.

CREDIT SUMMARY							
	PAYMENTS	BALANCES	LIMITS	TRADES	30+	60+	90+
REVOLVING	0	2061	2200	4	4	4	17
INSTALLMENT 1307	1307	79365	90610	25	34	8	27
REAL ESTATE	378	35384	36600	1	2	0	0
OPEN/OTHER	991	1041	1041	5	0	0	0
TOTAL	2676	117851	129451	38	40	12	44

# INQUIRIES 50	# PUBLIC RECORDS 0	# BANKRUPTCIES	0
WORST TRADE 9	OLDEST DATE 07/01/89	# SATISFACTORIES	17

SCORING

8   BEACON SCORE   EFX01
     519
     SERIOUS DELINQUENCY AND DEROGATORY PUBLIC RECORD OR COLLECTION FILED
     AMOUNT OWED ON DELINQUENT ACCOUNTS
     PROPORTION OF BALANCES TO CREDIT LIMITS TOO HIGH ON REVOLVING ACCOUNTS
     LENGTH OF TIME ACCOUNTS HAVE BEEN ESTABLISHED

8   EMPIRICA SCORE   TRU01
     493
     SERIOUS DELINQUENCY, AND PUBLIC RECORD OR COLLECTION FILED
     LEVEL OF DELINQUENCY ON ACCOUNTS
     TIME SINCE DELINQUENCY IS TOO RECENT OR UNKNOWN
     PROPORTION OF REVOLVING BALANCES TO REVOLVING CREDIT LIMITS IS TOO HIGH

8   FAIR ISAAC SCORE   XPN01
     529
     SERIOUS DELINQUENCY AND PUBLIC RECORD OR COLLECTION FILED
     PROPORTION OF BALANCES TOO HIGH ON REVOLVING ACCOUNTS
     NUMBER OF ACCOUNTS DELINQUENT
     LENGTH OF TIME SINCE LEGAL ITEM FILED OR COLLECTION ITEM REPORTED

The data included in this area may serve as verification data.

This area is not always as up-to-date as the data you will have available directly from the homeowner.

CREDIT HISTORY

ECOA	CREDITOR ACCOUNT NO	DATE RPTED	DATE LAST ACT	DATE OPND	LIMIT / HIGHEST CREDIT	PRESENT STATUS BALANCE OWING	AMOUNT PAST DUE	TERMS	PAY AMT	TYPE AND ACCT STATUS	HISTORICAL STATUS NO MOS HIIST REV	30	60	90
8	AFM-BLOOM #APRINTLO COLLEC CLOSED – CONS	02/99	04/94		425	425				OPN05 132111111 TRU01				
8	BENEFICL-HFC #7101702 CLOSED	07/00	04/00	03/97	0	0	0	39M 125		INS 01	37 XX1111111X1111111111X XXX11111111111111111 TRU01	0	0	0
8	CAPTIAL 1 BK 05291071382 CLOSED – CONS	04/00	01/00	06/96	592	0	0			REV01	41 111111111111111111111 111111111111111111111 TRU01	0	0	0
8	CCB 42270972 CREDIT CARD CREDIT CARD	07/00	02/00	07/98	950	0				REV01	24 EFX01	0	0	0
1	CITIBANK 54241800 CREDIT CARD	06/00	06/00	12/99	3500	3516	0	72	72	REV01	8 11111111 TRU01	0	0	0
8	CORNER STONE S0000070010 CLOSED AUTO	09/00	06/96	09/94	4374	0	0	18M 223		INS00	1 TRU01	0	0	0
8	DIRECT MERCH BK 54580000114 CREDIT CARD	07/00	07/00	11/95	2600	2496		83	83	REV01	25 111111111111111111111 111111111111111111111 XPN01	0	0	0
1	FCNB/NEWP 4220507 CHARGE ACCOUNT	07/00	06/00	09/99	900	888		30	30	REV01	10 111111111111111111111 111111111111111111111 TRU01	0	0	0
3	FIRST USA BANK NA 5417623 CREDIT CARD	07/00	07/00	12/99	3000	2602	0	65	65	REV01	8 11111111 TRU01	0	0	0
2	FNANB 15230035125 CREDIT CARD	09/00	09/00	12/99	3000	1976		79	79	REV01	9 111111111111111111111 11111 EPN01	0	0	0
1	FNANB VISA 54063555013	06/00	06/00	06/98	700	0				REV01	27 X1121111111111111111 EFX01	1	0	0

Credit History (12 months)
Homeowner

Mortgage Last 12 Months	Consumer Last 12 Months	Bankruptcy NOD/Foreclosure	Charge offs/Judgments
_____ X 30	_____ X 30	Chapter _____	# Filed _____
_____ X 60	_____ X 60	Discharge Date:	$ Amount _____
_____ X 90	_____ X 90	_____	$ to remain open _____
_____ X 120	_____ X 120	Balances: _____	$ to be paid _____
			_____ Credit Score

Credit History (12 months)
Secondary Homeowner

Mortgage Last 12 Months	Consumer Last 12 Months	Bankruptcy NOD/Foreclosure	Charge offs/Judgments
_____ X 30	_____ X 30	Chapter _____	# Filed _____
_____ X 60	_____ X 60	Discharge Date:	$ Amount _____
_____ X 90	_____ X 90	_____	$ to remain open _____
_____ X 120	_____ X 120	Balances: _____	$ to be paid _____
			_____ Credit Score

Figure7:8 Example Form – Credit Scoring

Credit History Scoring Key

You now have a better understanding of the inclusions of a credit report. You must learn to score each credit report to determine the workout options that may be available for each homeowner. The credit history-scoring key provides a simple method of extracting necessary information from the report and organizing the information for credit rating functions.

To begin the credit scoring process, you should locate the credit history-scoring key in the credit report section of your workbook. This key will assist you in organizing the information found in the credit report into a format that you can easily use when planning a workout plan for the homeowner.

➢ The first item of importance in the credit report is the mortgage history.

Locate the mortgage for the borrower's primary residence on the report.

Review the entries within the status segment to determine how many late payments exist over the last 12 to 24 months.

You will compare the homeowner's statement of hardship and explanation of the events that occurred to cause the default to the history illustrated on the credit report.

Example: If the homeowner has stated that the cause of the mortgage default is a rate adjustment and the adjustment occurred in June, all payments illustrated by the report prior to the June adjustment should be on time payments.

         If the credit report illustrates that the homeowner's history of late pays began before the date of the rate adjustment, a red flag will exist during the workout scrutiny.

When you are planning a workout strategy with the homeowner, you must ensure that all explanations match the documentary evidence.

If the borrower has additional real estate beyond their primary residence, you will need to determine how the loss mitigation guidelines require you to handle these housing payments. Most programs will define non-owner occupied mortgage payments as consumer credit rather than mortgage. A nonresident mortgage is often rated as consumer debt and you will need to rate the payments accordingly.

➤ Consumer history is the next field you will review.

You will tally all of late payments falling into the consumer debt category. These will include personal loans, credit card debt, revolving lines of credit, nonresident mortgage loans, and any other report items that indicate the borrower makes monthly payments toward the payment of a debt.

The history of the consumer debt should make sense when compared to the homeowner's explanation of the cause of the financial hardship that created the default situation.

When reviewing consumer debt, you will be primarily concerned with verifying the hardship explanation provided by the homeowner and determining if any matter exists that may create a lien against the subject property. A potential lien could place the loss mitigation workout plan in jeopardy.

➤ In addition to reviewing the body of the report to determine the status of the payments on each account, you will need to review the section relating to public records.

The public records field will contain information relating to any bankruptcy, foreclosure, or judgment against the homeowner.

You will typically become aware to look for these issues during the pre-qualification processes. The homeowner will usually define any derogatory debt that exists.

You should review the dates of all derogatory entries to determine if these may affect the lien position of the lender. Any judgment or subordinate lien against the subject property will need to be cleared under most loss mitigation workout plans.

At times, a derogatory debt may be showing in the columns that has been discharged as part of a bankruptcy proceeding.

If an item is showing on the report as an open account but has been discharged as part of a bankruptcy proceeding, you will need to obtain a credit supplement from the credit-reporting agency verifying that the debt is fully discharged.

You may also be required to submit full bankruptcy discharge paperwork as supporting documentation.

Early in your career, you may wish to complete a separate credit scoring form for each program until you become familiar with the requirements of each potential workout option.

Once you have completed all of the rating activity for the homeowner, you will follow the same rating system for the co-homeowner. You should be aware that joint accounts may be reported on both reports and be careful not to count these accounts twice during the scoring process.

If you tally an account twice, it will affect the debt to income ratio of the applicant, may affect the overall workout option.

It is sometimes beneficial to review the reports side by side and cross off any duplicate accounts on one of the reports, typically the co-homeowner's report.

Once you have completed the credit history-scoring key, the elements of the key will be compared to the workout options that are available for the homeowner.

CREDIT REPORT AUTHORIZATION AND RELEASE

Authorization is hereby granted to _____ to obtain a standard factual data credit report through a credit-reporting agency chosen by the _____.

My signature below authorizes the release to the credit-reporting agency a copy of my credit application, and authorizes the credit-reporting agency to obtain information regarding my employment, savings accounts, and outstanding credit accounts (mortgages, auto loans, personal loans, charge cards, credit unions, etc.) Authorization is further granted to the reporting agency to use a Photostatted reproduction of this authorization if necessary to obtain any information regarding the above-mentioned information.

Applicants hereby request a copy of the credit report with any possible derogatory information be sent to the address of present residence, and holds _____ and any credit reporting organization harmless in so mailing the copy requested.

Any reproduction of this credit authorization and release made by reliable means (for example, photocopy, or facsimile is considered an original.

_____
Homeowner's Signature
Date:
SSN:

_____
Homeowner's Signature
Date:
SSN:

_____
Homeowner's Signature
Date:
SSN:

_____
Homeowner's Signature
Date:
SSN:

Figure7:9 Credit Report Authorization and Release – HUD Release

Occupancy

Many lenders require that the property be owner occupied as the primary residence of the homeowner in order to consider many of the loss mitigation options.

> If the property is a second residence, vacation home, investment property or other form or non-owner occupied dwelling, many lenders will not enter into any loss mitigation plan except one that defines a repayment plan.

> Non-owner occupied repayment plans are typically not as liberal as those negotiated for the primary residence of the homeowner.

The most common repayment plan is one that requires the maintenance of all required payments on the date and in the amount stipulated in the loan note from the date of the plan forward.

In addition, a sustainable and acceptable recapture of the arrearages must be added to the monthly payment.

Some exceptions to the non-owner occupied negotiations may exist. If the file relates to a non-owner occupied property, you should complete the initial assessment form as you would with any new file. Upon completion of the initial assessment, you must review the guidelines of the lender or speak with your supervisor about potential negotiation option availability. These exceptions are set forth internally within the applicable lending institution and will vary greatly from case to case.

When the loss mitigation negotiations lead to a property retention plan, one aspect that will affect the approval is the use that the homeowner has been and intends to make of the property.

During the loss mitigation process, the homeowner will have provided information pertaining to the occupancy status of the property. It is a common practice to request that the homeowner to complete a statement in front of an authorized witness confirming these occupancy statements.

This occupancy declaration will be included in nearly every loss mitigation-closing package that results in the homeowner retaining possession of the property.

It is essential that you have confirmed the occupancy status of the property prior to remitting the initial negotiation package to the lender for review.

A negotiation closing could be stopped if the homeowner refuses to sign an occupancy declaration confirming that the property is the primary residence of the homeowner.

If you have conducted an adequate interview and completed the interview forms properly, this document will have a limited impact on the closing of the loss mitigation file.

OCCUPANCY DECLARATIONS

Lender:

RE: Loan No:
         PROPERTY ADDRESS:

The undersigned Borrower of the above described property does hereby declare, under penalty of perjury, as follows:

1.   Borrower shall occupy, establish, and use the Property as Borrowers principal residence within sixty days after execution of the Security Instrument and shall continue to occupy the property as Borrower's principal residence for at least one year after the date of occupancy unless Lender otherwise agrees in writing, which consent shall not be unreasonably withheld, or unless extenuating circumstances exist which are beyond the Borrower's control.

     You are hereby informed that Lender from time to time makes spot checks for owner occupancy on properties upon which we have secured a mortgage.

     Between the first and thirteenth day, after close of escrow, occupancy may be checked more than once. If after this check Lender is to believe that you never intended to occupy the subject as your primary residence, we may choose to call your note due and payable or increase your note rate by 100 basis points, in accordance with the applicable sections itemized on your note and Security Instrument and allowable by law.

2.   Borrower shall be in default, if during the loan application process, gave materially false or inaccurate information or statements to Lender (or failed to provide Lender with material information) in connection with the loan evidenced by the Note, including, but not limited to, representations concerning Borrower's occupancy of the Property as a Principal residence.

3.   The Lender has the right to foreclose on the loan under the terms of the Security Instrument if items 1 or 2 above are violated.

4.   Should Borrower's intention change prior to close of transaction, then it is agreed that the Lender will be immediately notified of that fact.

5.   Borrower understands that without this declaration of intention, Lender may not make the loan in connection with the property.

I DECLARE, UNDER PENALTY OF PERJURY, THAT THE FOREGOING DECLARATION IS TRUE AND CORRECT.

Figure7:10 - Sample Form – Occupancy Declaration – HUD Release

Term

Age / History Many lenders require that the loan be of a pre-specified age prior to the default activity.

What this means is that many lenders will require a proven history of making timely payments on the loan before they will consider entering into a loss mitigation negotiation.

> A common payment history requirement for a standard loan is 60 months or 5 years.

Those loans that were provided using an adjustable rate program may qualify under the lender's term criteria if the homeowner can illustrate that there was a history of timely payments prior to the first rate adjustment.

> Common rate adjustment terms are 1, 3, and 5 years.

Amortization The lender may negotiate a new amortization term as part of the loss mitigation negotiation process. The chapter relating to loan modification provides a foundation of knowledge regarding the manner in which amortization terms and interest rate change the situation of the homeowner. In addition to understanding how alteration to the loan terms can effect the required payment, you should gain an understanding of how the interest rate offered by the lender during negotiation is calculated.

CHAPTER

8

Property Value

*A comprehensive understanding of appraisals is
another vital area in which you must obtain
knowledge. Much of your training focuses on the
homeowner, their situation, and the loss mitigation
options available.*

*An important factor that everyone involved in the
transaction must consider is that the property is as
important as the homeowner in many of the loss
mitigation options.*

*The ability to provide a short sale offer, the principal
balance during a loan modification, a potential
refinance or short refinance transaction, and the
potential to sell the property within the current
market will all be based, in part, on the appraisal of
the property.*

When the homeowner applied for the loan, the lender had an appraisal completed to
determine the condition and value of the property securing the loan. When the loan is

granted, the homeowner is responsible for repaying the loan. The property acts as collateral, in the event the homeowner does not fulfill their obligations

Appraisals are essential to a variety of components of the loss mitigation process. The valuation and accuracy of an appraisal must be dependable. Appraisals will be used to help screen the homeowner's options under the loss mitigation process.

- Sales Price Negotiation in a Short Sale Transaction

- Loan-to-Value Assessment in a Refinance Transaction

- Principal Reduction Basis in a Loan Modification Transaction

- A determining of the property condition and potential repair cost

Not all loss mitigation negotiations will require that an appraisal be completed on the property. Some loss mitigation options, such as the forbearance, will not require an assessment of the property. Other loss mitigation negotiations, such as the short sale, will use the appraisal as the foundation for the negotiations.

The property value of the subject must be established before any of the higher-level loss mitigation options can be considered.

If the homeowner has a recent appraisal, you may wish to review the inclusions to determine any potential loss mitigation issues that may arise and to screen for possible loss mitigation resolutions. Any appraisal that you use as an assessment tools should be recent. The present market value of the property may not correlate to the previous value.

- Fluctuations in market conditions

- Surplus offerings in the market of the property

- Improvements to the property

- Other matters that affect the marketability

- Condition of the property

may all affect the value of the property.

UNIFORM RESIDENTIAL APPRAISAL REPORT

The purpose of this summary appraisal report is to provide with an accurate, and adequately supported opinion of market value of the subject property

Property Address	City	State Zip Code
Borrower Owner of Public Record		County

Legal Description

Assessor's Parcel #	Tax Year	R.E. Taxes $
Neighborhood Name	Map Reference	Census Tract

Occupant   Owner   Tenant   Vacant   Special Assessments $ PUD HOA $ per year   per month

Property Rights Appraised   Fee Simple   Leasehold   Other (describe)

Assignment Type   Purchase Transaction   Refinance Transaction   Other (describe)

Lender Client   Address

Is the subject property currently offered for sale or has it been offered for sale in the twelve months prior to the effective date of this appraisal   yes   no

Report data source(s) used offering prices(s), and date(s)

I   did   did not analyze the contract for sale for the subject purchase transaction. Explain the results of the analysis of the contract for sale or why analysis was not performed.

Contract Price $ Date of Contract   Is the property seller the owner of public record   Yes   No Data Source(s)

Is there any financial assistance (loan charges, sale concessions, gift or down payment assistance, etc.) to be paid by any party on behalf of the borrower?   Yes   No If yes, report the total dollar amount and describe the items to be paid.

Note: Race and racial composition of the neighborhood are not appraisal factors

Neighborhood Characteristics				One-Unit Housing Trends				One-Unit Housing	Present Land Use %	
Location	Urban	Suburban	Rural	Property Values	Increasing	Stable	Declining	PRICE AGE	One-Unit	%
Built-Up	Over 75%	25-75%	Under 25%	Demand Supply	Shortage	In Balance	Over Supply	$ (000) (yrs)	2-4 Unit	%
Growth	Rapid	Stable	Slow	Marketing Time	Under 2 mth	3-6 mths	Over 6 mths	Low	Multi-Family	%
Neighborhood Boundaries								High	Commercial	%
								Pred.	Other	%

Neighborhood Description

Market Conditions (including support for the above conclusions)

Dimension	Area	Shape	View

Specific Zoning Classification   Zoning Description

Zoning Compliance   Legal   Legal Nonconforming (Grandfathered use)   No Zoning   Illegal (describe)

Is the highest and best use of the subject property as improved (or as proposed per plans and specifications) the present use?   Yes   No If No, describe

Utilities   Public   Other (describe)   Public   Other (describe)   Off-site Improvements – Type   Public
Private

Electricity			Water			Street		
Gas			Sanitary Sewer			Alley		

FEMA Special Hazard Area   Yes   No FEMAL Flood Zone   Fema Map #   FEMA Map Date

Are the utilities and off-site improvements typical for the market area   Yes   No If No, describe

Are there any adverse site conditions or extreme factors (easements, encroachments, environmental conditions and uses, etc.)?   Yes   No If Yes, describe

General Description	Foundation	Exterior Description materials/condition	Interior materials/condition
Units One One w Accessory Unit	Concrete Slab Crawl Space	Foundation Walls	Floors
# of Stories	Full Basement Partial Basement	Exterior Walls	Walls
Type Det Att S-Dec / EndUnit	Basement Area sq ft	Roof Surface	Trim/Finish
Existing Proposed Under Cons	Basement Finish %	Gutters & Downspouts	Bath Floor
Design (Style)	Outside Entry/ Exist Sump Pump	Window Type	Bath Wainscot
Year Built	Evidence of Infestation	Storm Sash / Insulated	Car Storage None
Effective Age (Yrs)	Dampness Settlement	Screens	Driveway # of Cars
Attic None	Heating FWA HWBB Radiant	Amenities Woodstove(s)	Driveway Surface
Drop Stair Stairs	Other Fuel	Fireplaces # Fence	Garage # of Cars
Floor Scuttle	Cooling Central Air Conditioning	Patio/Deck Porch	Carport # of Cars
Finished Heated	Individual Other	Pool Other	Att Det Built-in
Appliances Refrigerator Range/Oven Dishwasher Disposal Microwave Washer/Dryer Other (describe)			

Finished area above grade contains: Rooms   Bedrooms   Bath(s)   Square Feet of Gross Living Area Above Grade

Additional Features (special energy efficient items, etc.)

Describe the conditions of the property (including needed repairs, deterioration, renovations, remodeling, etc.)

Are there any physical deficiencies or adverse conditions that affect the livability, soundness, or structural integrity of the property?   Yes   No If Yes, describe

Figure 8:1 - Sample Form – URAR – HUD Release

Subject

Property Address		City	State	Zip Code
Borrower	Owner of Public Record		County	
Legal Description				
Assessor's Parcel #		Tax Year	R.E. Taxes $	
Neighborhood Name		Map Reference	Census Tract	
Occupant ___ Owner ___ Tenant ___ Vacant	Special Assessments $	PUD HOA $ ____ per year ____ per month		
Property Rights Appraised ___ Fee Simple ___ Leasehold ___ Other (describe)				
Assignment Type ___ Purchase Transaction ___ Refinance Transaction ___ Other (describe)				
Lender Client		Address		
Is the subject property currently offered for sale or has it been offered for sale in the twelve months prior to the effective date of this appraisal ___ yes ___ no				
Report data source(s) used offering prices(s), and date(s)				

Figure 8:2 - Sample Form – URAR Extraction – HUD Release

The upper portion of the URAR contains identifying data, general details of the property being assessed, and information relating to the individuals involved in the transaction.

You should compare the details of this section to the information contained within the loss mitigation files. If any discrepancy between the appraisal report and your file details exists, you should ensure that the error or variation is corrected before submitting the appraisal. You should compare the

- Property Address

- Borrower Name

- Legal Description

- Owner of Public Record

- Assessor's Parcel Number

  Tax Year

  Real Estate Tax Amount

- Neighborhood Name

  Map Reference

  Census Tract

should match the loss mitigation data sheet entries. If a discrepancy exists, you must have the incorrect document corrected. Some of these details will be used to create the loan closing documents and having correct details ensures that all of the paperwork is correct and helps to stabilize the lender's security in the property.

The details relating to the occupancy refer to the present occupancy status of the property.

- Occupancy of the Property

    Owner
    Tenant
    Vacant

* Occupancy could become a red flag issue in the loss mitigation negotiation. Many lenders will only consider some of the higher-level loss mitigation options if the property is the primary residence of the homeowner. If the property is a second home, vacation home or investment property, the lender may decline all negotiations except a repayment plan.

The area relating to special assessments will be important to the loan.

- Special Assessments
    PUD
    HOA
    Terms

** You should ensure that any special assessments noted by the appraiser that are recurring costs are entered into the transaction costs. These assessments will become a factor in certain workout plans. The homeowner will be responsible for proving that these assessments are paid current during some of the loss mitigation options. If special assessments exist and the homeowner has not made payment, the payment of these items may become an issue during the loss mitigation negotiations.

The appraiser will define the rights being appraised. This section of the URAR refers to the rights that are available for transfer by the current owner of the property.

Property Rights Appraised

    Fee Simple
    Leasehold
    Other

The rights being transferred through the transaction may alter the security and potential loss mitigation options available to the homeowner.

If you note an error in a document, you must determine which document contains the error. If it is simple typing error or name entry method, the error can be easily corrected by the individual responsible for creating the document. If it is a more serious error, such as one relating to special assessments, you should re-assess the planned workout to ensure that the borrowers are still able to qualify for the planned workout.

CONTRACT

I __ did __ did not analyze the contract for sale for the subject purchase transaction. Explain the results of the analysis of the contract for sale or why analysis was not performed.
Contract Price $ Date of Contract   Is the property seller the owner of public record __ Yes __ No Data Source(s)
Is there any financial assistance (loan charges, sale concessions, gift or down payment assistance, etc.) to be paid by any party on behalf of the borrower? __ Yes __ No If yes, report the total dollar amount and describe the items to be paid.

Figure 8:3 - Sample Form – URAR Extraction – HUD Release

An appraisal request for use in a loss mitigation transaction will typically not include a contract. If the loss mitigation negotiation leads to a short sale transaction, the details of the sales contract presented by the qualified buyer will be included in any appraisal completed in relationship to the transaction.

Data pertaining to any sales contract or other contract that is a part of the transaction will be included within this section.

You will wish to supply a copy of the contract to the appraiser at the time of the appraisal request.

The appraiser will note whether the details of the contract were or were not reviewed during the completion of the appraisal.

- Contract Price

- Date of Contract

- Confirmation of Seller

- Financial Assistance

  Seller Concessions

Gift Funds
Down payment Assistance

You should review the financial details that the appraiser enters into the appraisal report including details relating to seller concessions, down payment assistance, and gift funds. The appraiser will take these details from the sales agreement. You should ensure that these inclusions match those that you incorporated into your workout plan.

Neighborhood

Neighborhood Characteristics				One-Unit Housing Trends				One-Unit Housing		Present Land Use %		
Location	Urban	Suburban	Rural	Property Values	Increasing	Stable	Declining	PRICE	AGE	One-Unit		%
Built-Up	Over 75%	25-75%	Under 25%	Demand Supply	Shortage	In Balance	Over Supply	$ (000)	(yrs)	2-4 Unit		%
Growth	Rapid	Stable	Slow	Marketing Time	Under 2 mth	3-6 mths	Over 6 mths	Low		Multi-Family		%
Neighborhood Boundaries								High		Commercial		%
								Pred.		Other		%
Neighborhood Description												

Figure 8:4 - Sample Form – URAR Extraction – HUD Release

Neighborhood Information

Details concerning the neighborhood of the property will be considered during the appraisal process.

Each line of the neighborhood assessment should be completed by the appraiser. There should be no blank lines or unchecked boxes. If an area is incomplete, you should contact the appraiser and request that they make the appropriate notations on the report before you submit the package to underwriting for review.

Assessments within the neighborhood section present vital information that may effect the loss mitigation negotiation.

Any variance from a positive answer or an uncommon answer should be scrutinized.

The loss mitigation specialist should note any neighborhood information that may affect the marketability of the property if a surrender option is being considered.

The homeowner may have less reason to maintain mortgage payments in a neighborhood that is degenerating so a negative neighborhood assessment may require additional scrutiny to determine if there is a possibility that the homeowner is attempting to enter loss mitigation negotiations in an attempt to walk away from the property.

Market Characteristics and Conditions

The appraiser will provide an assessment of market comparison and market conditions. You should review the appraiser's comments. Any comment that could be considered a negative factor may affect the workout plan approval. If the appraiser states that the market for property similar to the subject property is below average, the loss mitigation department may be less likely to approve certain workout options.

SITE

Dimension	Area	Shape	View
Specific Zoning Classification	Zoning Description		
Zoning Compliance Legal Legal Nonconforming (Grandfathered use) No Zoning Illegal (describe)			
Is the highest and best use of the subject property as improved (or as proposed per plans and specifications) the present use? Yes No If No, describe			
Utilities Public Other (describe)	Public Other (describe)	Off-site Improvements – Type Public Private	
Electricity	Water	Street	
Gas	Sanitary Sewer	Alley	
FEMA Special Hazard Area Yes No FEMAL Flood Zone	Fema Map #	FEMA Map Date	
Are the utilities and off-site improvements typical for the market area Yes No If No, describe			
Are there any adverse site conditions or extreme factors (easements, encroachments, environmental conditions and uses, etc.)? Yes No If Yes, describe			

Figure 8:5 - Sample Form – URAR Extraction – HUD Release

The site segment of the appraisal describes the parcel on which the subject property is built and any issue regarding site usage that are apparent.

Any issues with the use of the land including easements, encroachment, boundary line issues, or other factors affecting the land should be reviewed and addressed. Issues affecting the use of the land may need to be corrected before the loss mitigation workout can be finalized. Guidelines will dictate what generates a red flag stipulation regarding site and site usage.

Improvements

General Description	Foundation	Exterior Description materials/condition	Interior materials/condition
Units One One w Accessory Unit	Concrete Slab Crawl Space	Foundation Walls	Floors
# of Stories	Full Basement Partial Basement	Exterior Walls	Walls
Type Det Att S-Dec / End Unit	Basement Area sq ft	Roof Surface	Trim/Finish
Existing Proposed Under Cons	Basement Finish %	Gutters & Downspouts	Bath Floor
Design (Style)	Outside Entry/ Exist Sump Pump	Window Type	Bath Wainscot
Year Built	Evidence of Infestation	Storm Sash / Insulated	Car Storage None
Effective Age (Yrs)	Dampness Settlement	Screens	Driveway # of Cars
Attic None	Heating FWA HWBB Radiant	Amenities Woodstove(s)	Driveway Surface
Drop Stair Stairs	Other Fuel	Fireplaces # Fence	Garage # of Cars
Floor Scuttle	Cooling Central Air Conditioning	Patio/Deck Porch	Carport # of Cars
Finished Heated	Individual Other	Pool Other	Att Det Built-in
Appliances Refrigerator Range/Oven Dishwasher Disposal Microwave Washer/Dryer Other (describe)			
Finished area above grade contains: Rooms Bedrooms Bath(s) Square Feet of Gross Living Area Above Grade			
Additional Features (special energy efficient items, etc.)			
Describe the conditions of the property (including needed repairs, deterioration, renovations, remodeling, etc.)			

Figure 8:6 - Sample Form – URAR Extraction – HUD Release

Many of the red flags that occur with an appraisal review will occur in the area of the appraisal that relates to the improvements. The term improvement refers to the actual building of the property. All portions of the subject property should obtain at least a rating of average.

If the property rating is less than average, the homeowner and the lender will need to negotiate the handling of any steps that will be taken to improve the rating of the property.

A new purchaser in a short sale transaction may not be able to secure financing on the property until negative matters have been addressed.

The appraiser will check the boxes that relate to the property.

# of Units   These will include the number of units contained within the subject property. You should ensure that the number of units reflected on the appraisal is the same as the number of units indicated on the workout sheet.

# of Stories   The number of stories included in the property will affect the desirability of the property. The comparables used for the valuation portion of the appraisal should be of a similar number of stories.

Status   The appraiser will note the status of the property including whether the improvements are existing, under construction or planned improvements.

Design   The design of the property will affect the desirability of the property. The comparables used for the valuation portion of the appraisal should be of a similar design and appeal.

Year Built/
Age   The year that the property was built and the effective age of the property will affect the value. The year built is the actual age. Improvements, renovations, and updating are factored into the effective age. A home may be a number of decades old and have a much younger effective age if the property has been renovated to bring it into line with newer construction.

Attic   The inclusion or exclusion of an attic may affect both the desirability and the value of a property. Square foot value is typically assessed to those areas that are heated and cooled. These areas are considered to be living square feet. If the attic is used as living square feet, it will be factored as part of the dollar per square foot valuation process. If the attic is used for storage and does not qualify as living square footage, it will still be a factor during underwriting, but more often as a determination that the property of similar design and appeal as the comparables used during the valuation processes.

Foundation The type of foundation, including the type of basement that they property contains will effect both the desirability and the value of the property. Similar to an attic, a finished basement with a heat source may be considered as living square footage and factored as part of the dollar per square foot valuation. A basement used as storage will be apply as a determination that the subject property is of a similar design and appeal as the comparables used during the valuation process.

Issues The appraiser will note any issues that are apparent in the basement area of the property. Any issues, including dampness, infestation, or settlement of the property may need to be addressed before the workout plan can be finalized. These issues may put the value and condition of the property at risk if left unaddressed.

Heating / Cooling The type of heating and cooling contained within the subject property may affect the value and appeal of the property. The comparables used for valuation should contain a similar type of heating and cooling sources as the subject property.

Exterior/ Interior The interior and exterior of the property should be in good condition. The appraiser will confirm that there is not a large discrepancy between the materials of the subject property and the materials of the comparable properties. The loss mitigation department will be most interested in the appraiser notes relating to condition. The condition rating set by the appraiser should be at least average. Any condition rating below average may need to be addressed before the workout can be finalized.

Amenities will add value to the property. The appraiser will note any special features or amenities relevant to the subject property.

Appliances The inclusion of appliances in the transfer of real estate is not a factor unless the value of the appliances equals a substantial amount of the overall value of a property or if the comparables do include a much greater number or quality of appliances in the transfer.

Square Feet The appraiser will enter the total square feet of the property and the number of rooms encompassed by this square footage. He will also note the number of these rooms that are bedrooms and bathroom space.

The appraiser will make adjustments during the valuation processes for the differences in square footage between the subject property and the comparable property. The appraiser will also make adjustments based on the use of the square footage.

Comment The URAR form provides the appraiser with an area to provide opinion about the property. This option section has places available to comment on

- Additional features of the property

- Condition of the property including items that

  o presently require repairs
  o are in a state of deterioration
  o are undergoing renovations
  o have other apparent issues that the appraiser feels may affect the value of the property

- Deficiencies that affect the livability, soundness or structural integrity of the property

- Neighborhood in comparison to the subject property

The appraiser will enter any comments that they feel are important to the ability of the subject property to maintain its present value. If any item is defined within the comments area that creates a potential for a loss in value, the lending loss mitigation department may require that the issue be cured or corrected, before the workout plan can be approved and finalized.

You will want to review each entry within the Improvements Comment section and ensure you understand the problems that may arise. You will also wish to inform any applicable parties to the transaction about the comments.

We recommend contacting your appraiser if you note a discrepancy, error, or issue on the appraisal report. This recommendation does not indicate that you should influence the appraiser's decision and comments in any manner.

The purpose of the contact is to confirm the information in the URAR is correct according to the appraiser's record.

The only alterations you should request to a completed appraisal are alterations arising because of an error or omission.

You should never attempt to influence or alter the opinion of the appraiser.

UNIFORM RESIDENTIAL APPRAISAL REPORT

There are	comparable properties currently offered for sale in the subject neighborhood ranging in price from $					to $		
There are	comparable sales in the subject neighborhood within the past twelve months ranging in sales price from $					to $		
FEATURE	SUBJECT	COMPARABLE SALE #1		COMPARABLE SALE #2		COMPARABLE SALE #3		
Address								
Proximity to Subject								
Sale Price	$	$		$		$		
Sale Price/Gross Liv Area	$ sq ft	$ sq ft		$ sq ft		$ sq ft		
Data Source(s)								
Verification Source(s)								
VALUE ADJUSTMENTS	DESCRIPTION	DESCRIPTION	Adjustment	DESCRIPTION	Adjustment	DESCRIPTION	Adjustment	
Sales or Financing Concessions								
Date of Sale / Time								
Location								
Leasehold/Fee Simple								
Site								
View								
Design (Style)								
Quality of Construction								
Actual Age								
Condition								
Above Grade Room Count	Total Bdrms Baths	Total Bedrms Baths		Total Brms Baths		Total Brms Baths		
Gross Living Area	sq ft	sq ft		sq ft		sq ft		
Basement & Finished Rooms Below Grade								
Functional Utility								
Heating / Cooling								
Energy Efficient								
Garage / Carport								
Porch/Patio/Deck								
Net Adjustment		+ -	$	+ -	$	+ -	$	
Adjusted Sales Price of Comps		Net Adj % Gross Adj %	$	Net Adj % Gross Adj %	$	Net Adj % Gross Adj %	$	
I __did__ did not research the sale or transfer history of the subject property and comparable sales. If not, explain								
My research __did__ did not reveal any prior sales or transfers of the subject property for the three years prior to the effective date of this appraisal.								
Data source(s)								
My research __did__ did not reveal any prior sales or transfers of the comparables sales for the year prior to the date of sale of the comparable sale.								
Data source(s)								
Report the results of the research and analysis of the prior sale or transfer history of the subject property and comparable sales (report additional on pg 3)								

Kenney

ITEM	SUBJECT	COMPARABLE SALE #1	COMPARABLE SALE #2	COMPARABLE SALE #3
Date of Prior Sale/Transfer				
Price of Prior Sale/Transfer				
Data Source(s)				
Effective Date of Data Source(s)				

Analysis of prior sale or transfer history of the subject property and comparable sales

Summary of Sales Comparison Approach

Indicated Value by Sales Comparison Approach $

Indicated Value by: Sales Comparison Approach $	Cost Approach (if developed) $	Income Approach (if developed)$

The appraisal is made __ as is __ subject to completion per plans and specifications on the basis of a hypothetical condition that the improvements have been completed. __ subject to the following repairs or alterations on the basis of a hypothetical condition that repairs have been completed, or __ subject to the following required inspection based on the extraordinary assumption that the condition or deficiency does not require alteration or repair.

Figure 8:7 - Sample Form – URAR – HUD Release

Comparable Valuation

There are	comparable properties currently offered for sale in the subject neighborhood ranging in price from $ to $
There are	comparable sales in the subject neighborhood within the past twelve months ranging in sales price from $ to $

FEATURE	SUBJECT	COMPARABLE SALE #1		COMPARABLE SALE #2		COMPARABLE SALE #3	
Address							
Proximity to Subject							
Sale Price	$	$		$		$	
Sale Price/Gross Liv Area	$ sq ft	$ sq ft		$ sq ft		$ sq ft	
Data Source(s)							
Verification Source(s)							
VALUE ADJUSTMENTS	DESCRIPTION	DESCRIPTION	Adjustment	DESCRIPTION	Adjustment	DESCRIPTION	Adjustment
Sales or Financing Concessions							
Date of Sale / Time							
Location							
Leasehold/Fee Simple							
Site							
View							
Design (Style)							
Quality of Construction							
Actual Age							
Condition							
Above Grade Room Count	Total Bdrms Baths	Total Bedrms Baths		Total Brms Baths		Total Brms Baths	
Gross Living Area	sq ft	sq ft		sq ft		sq ft	
Basement & Finished Rooms Below Grade							
Functional Utility							
Heating / Cooling							
Energy Efficient							
Garage / Carport							
Porch/Patio/Deck							
Net Adjustment		+ -	$	+ -	$	+ -	$
Adjusted Sales Price of Comps		Net Adj % Gross Adj %	$	Net Adj % Gross Adj %	$	Net Adj % Gross Adj %	$

Figure 8:8 - Sample Form – URAR Extraction – HUD Release

157

Page two of the URAR will contain the valuation and cost analysis the appraiser completes when assessing the value of the property. The cost analysis may take two forms either the Cost Approach or the Sales Comparison Approach.

You will see the sales comparison approach used more frequently within your files than the cost approach.

The sales comparison data assesses the characteristics and condition of the subject property as compared to other, similar properties sold within a given time period and in the same area as the subject property. The property should be

- Similar in design and appeal as the subject property

- Similar in size and condition as the subject property

- Similar in features and amenities as the subject property

- Similar in site design, use, and view as the subject property

- Within a defined distance of the subject property

    Example: Within the same neighborhood

- Sold within a pre-set time limit of the date of the appraiser

If a comparable property included on the appraisal does not meet one of these qualifications, the appraiser will need to explain the reason that the comparable was selected as a data source.

Example: Rural property often exceeds the distance requirement as the mass of land encompassed by rural property often makes it difficult to locate many pieces of sold property within the same neighborhood and within the sales time limit.

At times, underwriting may require additional actions if the comparables used by the appraiser do not meet the standards set within the guidelines of the loan program. Common stipulations that relate to an unacceptable data source inclusion would be to request two additional comparables be incorporated into the appraisal or that an appraisal field review be conducted to verify the value and other information included within the original appraisal.

The subject property will be compared to each of the comparables selected by the appraiser.

Proximity The distance between the properties being compared effects the value.

The appraiser should locate similar properties sold within a reasonable time that are close in location to the subject property.

Property values vary greatly from one neighborhood to the next. It is important that property comparisons use properties that are located in similarly valued areas.

A comparable property that exceeds reasonable proximity guidelines as set by underwriting for your loan program will require an explanation by the appraiser.

Additional comparables may be needed to validate the value indicated within the appraisal.

Sales Price The sales price of the comparables is the starting basis that will be used to determine the value of your subject property.

The factors listed below sales price will increase or decrease the value of the subject property in comparison with other closed sales in the area.

Any area of the subject property that is lacking as compared to the comparison properties will result in a decrease to the sales price baseline of the comparable.

Any area of the subject property that is a positive as compared to the comparison properties will result in an increase to the sales price baseline of the comparable.

Sales Price /
Gross Living A dollar figure will be determined for the cost per square foot of the comparable property.

This figure is determined by dividing the total sales price by the total square foot of each property.

Data Sources   The appraiser will note the source from which they obtained each entry included in the appraisal.

The comparable property sales price will be adjusted based on comparison factors between the subject property and the comparable property. Each of these adjustment items will result in a change in the price valuation.

Concessions   Any concession relating to the transfer of the comparison property will be included as part of the appraisal. These concessions may alter the transaction through an increase in overall value.

These will not be common elements of the loss mitigation appraisal but may appear on an appraisal that is updated or generated during a short sale or other transfer transaction.

Date of Sale   A date that is too far removed (past) will need to be addressed.

The date of the sale of the comparison property helps to define the accuracy of the value estimate. The real estate market has undergone dramatic value shifts recently and a sale from six months ago may not reflect the value of a property today. A date that is too far removed (past) will need to be addressed.

At times, the appraiser may exceed the time limitations set by the loss mitigation guidelines. This exception could occur for a variety of reasons including a slow market in which very few homes have transferred or a neighborhood that contains an exceptionally high number of long-term residences and few property transfers.

The appraiser should include an explanation regarding any property sale used for comparison purposes that exceeds the sale date requirements.

Location   An assessment of average or above is desired with regard to property location.

The property values between neighborhoods can vary dramatically. Any exceptional variance in location may indicate that the value of the appraisal is not correct.

Any assessment below average will need to be addressed.

This may be a red flag.

Any assessment that indicates the property is located in a below average or deteriorating neighborhood may generate additional scrutiny and questions from the lender. A deteriorating neighborhood is one of the causes of a homeowner choosing to surrender the property and walk away from the transaction. Many lenders will decline any loss mitigation offer from a homeowner who is entering loss mitigation in an attempt to dispose of a devalued or over financed property.

Site Size   The sites should be similar in size. A large difference between the land included with the transfer of the subject property and a comparable property will need to be addressed.

A variance between the site sizes of the properties will result in an alteration to the value. Most program guidelines have specific parameters regarding the percentage of the overall property value allocated to the land and the percentage allocated to improvements, setting very specific limits on the amount of the overall value that may be allocated to the land.

This issue typically arises in the transfer of rural property.

The differences relating to site size may generate additional scrutiny and questions from the lender. A smaller site size than average may make marketing a property for sale difficult or result in a decrease is value for the property. An unusual site size for the neighborhood is one of the causes of a homeowner choosing to surrender the property and walk away from the transaction. Many lenders will decline any loss mitigation offer from a homeowner who is entering loss mitigation in an attempt to dispose of a devalued or over financed property.

View   The sites should be of similar rating concerning view assessment.

A difference in the assessment of the view level between the properties may result in an alteration in the value of the subject property.

A rating of a below average view may generate additional scrutiny and questions from the lender. A property whose view has been compromised because of changes in the neighborhood is one of the causes of a homeowner choosing to surrender the property and walk away from the transaction. Many lenders will decline any loss mitigation offer from a homeowner who is entering loss mitigation in an attempt to dispose of a devalued or over financed property.

Design / Style

The properties should be of similar design and appeal levels. A difference in the design and style of the properties will require an explanation by the appraiser. The appraiser will need to define the reason that they chose a comparable property of a different design or style than the subject.

Quality of Const

The properties should be of similar quality. Any difference in the quality levels of the property will need to be explained by the appraiser.

An entry of below average construction may generate additional scrutiny and questions from the lender. A property that is of poor quality construction may be deteriorating. This is one of the causes of a homeowner choosing to surrender the property and walk away from the transaction. Many lenders will decline any loss mitigation offer from a homeowner who is entering loss mitigation in an attempt to dispose of a devalued or over financed property.

Age of Property

The properties used for comparison purposes should be similar to the age of the subject property. The age of a property affects its value and the appraiser will need to define the reason that the comparables used as data sources are of a different age basis than the subject property.

Room Count /Square Ft

The room counts and square footage of the properties should be similar.

A difference in the room count between the subject property and the comparable property will result in a change to the value assessment assigned by the appraiser.

Underwriting may require additional actions or explanations relating to the differences in property room count.

The dollar value per square foot calculations will be completed by the appraiser. These act as a baseline for the other value calculations. A large discrepancy in square footage between the subject property and the comparison property will alter the value assessed by the appraiser.

Basement The size and use of the basement of the subject property and comparable properties should be similar. If the basement of the subject property is finished, the basement area of the comparable properties should also be finished.

A variance between the properties will result in an alteration in value.

Functional Utility The functional utility of all of the properties should be similar. A difference in the functional utility of the subject property from the comparables will require an explanation by the appraiser.

A difference in the quality of construction may result in an alteration in the value allowed by underwriting.

The subject property should obtain an assessment of at least average. Any entry of below average may generate additional scrutiny and questions from the lender. A property that has a lower functional assessment may limit the value and marketability of the property. This is one of the causes of a homeowner choosing to surrender the property and walk away from the transaction. Many lenders will decline any loss mitigation offer from a homeowner who is entering loss mitigation in an attempt to dispose of a devalued or over financed property.

Heating / Cooling The heating and cooling systems of the properties will need to be similar.

A difference between the types or inclusion of heating or cooling systems may result in an alteration in value. The type of heating and cooling systems may not be a red flag depending on the region and the commonality of the various heating and cooling systems in use. The addition or exclusion of a cooling system or the age of the heating and cooling system may be a factor.

Energy
Efficient   The properties should be of similar levels of energy efficiency.

A large discrepancy in the energy efficiency levels of the properties may result in an alteration in value. The subject property must obtain a rating of at least average. A rating of below average will need to be addressed.

This may be a red flag.

Garage /
Carport   The inclusion of a garage or carport should be similar between all properties. The appraiser will assess a value to the garage or carport. The comparison section of the appraisal should reflect the alteration in value that results from the inclusion or lack of a garage or carport in one of the properties.

If either the subject property or one of the comparables has or lacks a garage or carport and the other property does not, you should confirm that the value adjustments have been entered into the appropriate field by the appraiser. If there is no value adjustment relating to the inclusion or lack of a garage or carport, you should question the appraiser regarding the lack of an adjustment.

The appraisal may need to be modified to include this value change.

Porch /
Patio / Deck   The inclusion of a porch, patio, or deck should be similar between all properties. The appraiser will assess a value to the porch, patio, or deck. The comparison section of the appraisal should reflect the alteration in value that results from the inclusion or lack of a porch, patio, or deck in one of the properties.

If either the subject property or one of the comparables has or lacks a porch, patio, or garage and the other property does not, you should confirm that the value adjustments have been entered into the appropriate field by the appraiser.

If there is no value adjustment relating to the inclusion or lack of a porch, patio, or carport, you should question the appraiser regarding the lack of an adjustment.

Kenney

The appraisal may need to be modified to include this value change.

An alteration to this inclusion will result in an alteration in the value.

ITEM	SUBJECT	COMPARABLE SALE #1	COMPARABLE SALE #2	COMPARABLE SALE #3
Date of Prior Sale/Transfer				
Price of Prior Sale/Transfer				
Data Source(s)				
Effective Date of Data Source(s)				
Analysis of prior sale or transfer history of the subject property and comparable sales				

Figure 8:9 - Sample Form – URAR Extraction – HUD Release

Adjustments and Sales Price

Net Adjustments The net adjustments section is where the appraiser will add and subtract all of the alterations to the value between the comparable properties and the subject property.

Each item that the appraiser assesses for comparison between the properties will be assigned a value.

Any item that was lacking in the subject property but present in the comparison property will result in a reduction from the sales price of the comparable.

Any items that was lacking in the comparable but present in the subject will result in an increase to the sales price of the comparable.

Adjusted Sales Price The adjustments will then be added to or subtracted from the sales price of the comparable.

The resulting calculations of these adjustments the value that the appraiser believes the subject property would have or will be worth when offered for sale in the present market.

This is the comparison approach to property valuation.

Signature The signature of the appraiser indicates he has completed the appraiser and certifies that the market value of the property has been duly determined per appraiser guidelines.

Research and Comments

Comments   The comment section on this page will often address issues the appraiser encountered that may affect the value of the property or that will raise questions regarding the transfer of the property.

Review the comments to determine if the appraiser has addressed any additional red flags that may effect your transaction.

Analysis and Indicated Value

The appraiser will then place the value figure he has obtained through comparison and research on the appraisal page.

This is the final appraised value of the property.

COST APPROACH TO VALUE

The cost approach is used to determine value based upon the replacement cost of the subject property. It is not a typical approach to value that will be used for most loss mitigation negotiations or regular market value assessments for the purpose of listing a property for sale; however, the cost approach will provide important data regarding the reproduction or replacement of the subject property if such a result should become necessary.

INCOME APPROACH

The income approach to value will often be used for rental or other income producing property. The income approach uses many of the same data indicators as the core appraisal but adds the factor of income to the final value of the property.

PUD PROJECT INFORMATION

If the property is located in a Planned Unit Development (PUD), the final section will play a role in the final value determination. You should review this section for any additional issues that may become apparent if your transaction involves a PUD. These may include the need to determine the payment status on any assessments or fees assigned to the property.

SOLUTION QUICK LIST

Counseling   A homeowners who receives early credit counseling may be able to resume the payment of their mortgage debt by working out a financial budget, through negotiations on their revolving debt or by restructuring their spending habits.

If the initial interview indicates that the default is a result of a temporary cash flow matter or a disorganized budgeting system referring the homeowner to a credit services agency may enable the homeowner to gain baseline stability. This counseling may enable the homeowner to initiate a repayment strategy that that enhances the ability of your workout negotiations to succeed or removes the need for loss mitigation options entirely.

Forbearance   When the matter behind the default is temporary in nature with a corrective solution available in the near future, a forbearance plan may be put into place.

The forbearance plan enables the homeowner to take a temporary hiatus from the mortgage payment. The hiatus provides the time necessary for the homeowner to recover from the temporary financial set back and recapture the financial stability that existed before the default.

- Proof of Hardship

- Proof of Term

- Proof of ability to repay at conclusion of hardship

When you negotiate a forbearance plan, you must screen the homeowner's future financial repayment ability to determine the best repayment method for the homeowner.

Forgiveness   Proof of ability to resume basic P&I payments but expected financial situation illustrates an inability to pay any additional sums toward the arrears

Most lenders will only consider a forgiveness plan when the loan will go to complete default such as foreclosure, short sale or deed in lieu without the forgiveness and it can be proven that the homeowner will have the ability to resume the P&I Payments.

Payment Plus
Percentage: The most common forbearance repayment plan dictates that the homeowner will resume payments at the end of the forbearance at a rate of full P&I payments dictated by the note PLUS an additional monthly payment percentage to be allocated to the forbearance accumulations.

The negotiation of this plan requires a review of homeowners DTI, likely future earnings ability, and willingness to maintain the payment plus percentage plan.

Many lenders will begin negotiations at a repayment rate of 1 ½ times the regular mortgage payment.

You should screen the homeowner carefully to ensure that the repayment plan minimizes the likelihood of a recurring default but repays the arrears in a timely manner.

Refinance   A homeowner with adequate equity interest in the home through payment application, property condition increases, or market appreciation may be eligible for a traditional refinance.

The traditional refinance will follow the Guideline Matrix of the loan program for which the homeowner might qualify. Many traditional matrix will only consider a refinance if the credit history contains positive points. A homeowner who has not yet defaulted on a mortgage payment may be eligible under traditional refinance parameters. You should refer any early contact from a homeowner to a Loan Officer from a reputable lender. The lender will be able to complete a pre-qualification assessment for available loan programs.

Short Refinance   A short refinance is a refinance scenario where the homeowner may be able to refinance the rate, term, and principal balance of their mortgage even if blemishes already exist on the credit history. Most short refinance transactions will be completed under a governmental loan program or through the lender holding the default note.

A refinance within the lending institution holding the defaulted note that contains multiple changes will often fall within the category of a loan modification.

Loan Modification   Homeowners who had a good history of making payments on their mortgage prior to an unexpected occurrence may qualify for the loan modification program.

The loan modification dictates that a verifiable unforeseen event such as a job loss, rate adjustment, increase in living expense, or other matter must occur in the profile of the homeowner. This event must have had a financial impact that made the maintenance of the current mortgage payment impossible according to homeowner DTI ratio analysis.

The loan modification will enable the interest rate, loan term, principal balance, or other loan element to be changed if it is clear that the modification will result in the homeowner's capacity to maintain the newly defined mortgage terms.

Sale of Property   If the screening you complete indicates that the buyer does not have either the ability or the willingness to enter a retention program, a sale of the property should be considered.

The best case for sale is when the property has sufficient value or the homeowner has sufficient equity in the property to facilitate a sale.

If the sale of the property is a viable option but the homeowner is unable to meet the monthly payments required to keep the note current during the marketing of the property, a temporary forbearance or reduction in monthly payments may be negotiated. These reductions or payment delay options will be customized to meet the time on the market and sale data within the region.

The lender will stipulate minimum marketing requirements before entering into a forbearance or payment reduction agreement. These requirements include:

- Retention of a licensed real estate agent for sales assistance

- Sales price that correlates well to the present market not the homeowner's equity position or perceived property value

- Cooperation on the part of the homeowner in the sales process

- Effort on the part of the homeowner to enhance the marketability of the property including

> General maintenance
>
> Cosmetic repairs
>
> Possibly more elaborate repair to the property if the condition has fallen to sub-standard levels.

The requirements of the straight sale process are similar to the stipulations of the short sale proceedings except the lender will usually not lower the principal balance required to obtain a loan satisfaction.

The appraisal and market condition evaluation will dictate the ability to negotiate a straight sale forbearance or payment reduction.

Short Sale/PFS   If the equity position of the property or present market conditions does not indicate the likelihood that the homeowner will be able to market the property and obtain a purchase contract equal to or greater than the sums owed against the property, a short sale option may be negotiated.

To negotiate a short sale option, the lender must be willing to accept a loss on the principal amount of the loan.

The first step to obtaining an agreement to accept such a loss on the part of the lender is to prove the current market value of the property.

Market value is defined as the amount of money a reasonably informed buyer is willing to pay and a reasonably informed seller willing to accept to affect the transfer of an item.

In the case of real estate, the market value will be established by

Current appraised value

Comparable property sales data

Each of the loss mitigation strategies can be a stand-alone work out option or the strategies may be stacked to encompass multiple methods of working out the delinquency.

Example: Special forbearance may be combined with any reinstatement option including delinquent refinance. The combination of options will be sequential, not simultaneous.

Special forbearance may be used to reinstate a loan prior to an assumption.

Pre-foreclosure may be combined with a deed-in-lieu provision in the event the property does not sell within the time required.

Modification may be combined with a special forbearance to bring the loan current prior to the beginning of the new payment base

Sometimes the loss mitigation efforts will fail despite your best efforts. It is important that you

- screen each potential loss mitigation candidate carefully

- implement the best negotiation strategy for each situation

- ensure that the practices you follow during negotiation are above reproach

If you follow the guides of good negotiation technique and sound investigative strategy, the failure rate of your loss mitigation efforts will be minimized.

CHAPTER

9

Special Considerations

A loss mitigation specialist is a professional negotiator who assists a party involved in a default transaction in reaching a speedy and fair resolution to the situation.

> The primary goal of a loss mitigation specialist is to negotiate the elements of the transaction to minimize the loss to all parties, streamline the transfer processes, and create a workable loss mitigation plan.

Loss mitigation presents multiple options for each default situation. As a professional in the negotiation process, you will customize each element of the work out plan to suit the situation of the homeowner and the needs of the lender.

The flow of loss mitigation options should begin with the choice that will have the least long-term impact on the homeowner and minimize the losses to the lender.

You will begin the processes by conducting a comprehensive interview with the homeowner to gain an overview of the elements of their financial situation. These elements will dictate the potential loss mitigation options that may apply to their situation.

You will then begin to negotiation a work out plan that is customized to the needs of the homeowner.

Customizing the work out plan to the situation of each claim assists the homeowner in retaining homeownership but also provides the lender with the opportunity to minimize the financial impact of the foreclosure process.

The lender will have specific guidelines and screening parameters that will apply to each negotiation. Some lenders may be servicing loans that are insured through HUD. These loans carry a pre-set insurance premium or PMI that the homeowner pays to the mortgage lender as part of their monthly payment.

In exchange for the PMI premium, HUD provides a security to the lender that they will help offset the loss suffered by the lender in homeowner default situations. If the loan you are involved in negotiating is subject to PMI, HUD will have specific guidelines, disclosure requirements, negotiation maximums, and reporting requirements that the lender will follow in a loss mitigation negotiations. HUD insured loans might also contain guidelines for additional financial incentives for both the lender and the homeowner in exchange for certain work out options. These work out fees may be applied to the cost of negotiation and servicing on defaulted loan negotiations. If HUD applies to the default you are negotiating, you should first define the general parameters of the negotiation options and then review the HUD specific guidelines and requirements to ensure that you comply with each element. The lender may have a specific department, who is responsible for remitting necessary documents and disclosures, but the loss mitigation expert will be responsible for ensuring the financial negotiation and negotiation timelines comply with the regulations.

- Consider all reasonable means to address delinquency at the earliest possible moment.

- Inform homeowners of available loss mitigation options and the availability of housing counseling within the second month of delinquency.

- Evaluate each delinquent loan no later than the 90th day of delinquency to determine which loss mitigation option is appropriate.

- Use loss mitigation whenever feasible to avoid foreclosure.

- Re-evaluate each loan monthly until reinstatement or foreclosure.

- Initiate foreclosure within six months of default unless a loss mitigation option is being pursued and ensure that all actions taken are documented.

- Retain a complete audit trail confirming compliance with all loss mitigation requirements.

The use of loss mitigation tools are meant to provide a relief option to homeowners who are currently in default on mortgage payments. The term default dictates that at least one, and perhaps multiple, mortgage payments have not been made in compliance with the terms of the mortgage note.

Disaster Related Loss Mitigation Action
HUD Guidelines
Data Reference : HUD Release to Mortgage Lenders

Please note, the following guidelines has been obtained directly from HUD and included for illustrative purposes. Program availability, eligibility requirements, timelines, and other matters are subject to change at any time.

You should refer to the applicable HUD release to obtain the most up-to-date standards.

Homeowners with a property in a designated disaster area may be provided with exceptions relating to the standard loss mitigation processes and pre-requisite. The availability of these exceptions is based on the loan type. If the loan is insured through a government entity, HUD has additional assistance processes in place to assist these homeowners during recovery from the hardship created by the disaster.

The fundamental goal is to assist homeowners with property damaged during one of the designated major catastrophes in retaining possession of the home. The timeline and standards in place governing loss mitigation efforts geared toward homeowner retention enable an expanded use of the requisites detailed under the loan modification requirements. However, some property may be damaged beyond the ability of the homeowner to mitigate. When the property is damaged and will not be repaired, HUD has established enhanced deed-in-lieu of foreclosure processes for loans that fall under their prevue.

When the President declares a disaster, certain mortgage related actions and exceptions are in place to assist the homeowner. The loss mitigation specialist must check with the Federal Emergency Management Agency (FEMA) to obtain the specific affected counties and corresponding declaration dates and refer to the most recent program exception updates.

Figure 9:1 - Data Reference : HUD Release to Mortgage Lenders

Kenney

Mortgage Insurance for Disaster Victims

HUD has a special mortgage insurance program under to assist disaster victims. Under this program, a homeowner whose residence was destroyed or damaged to such an extent that reconstruction or replacement is necessary are eligible for 100 percent financing.

The previous residence must have been in the disaster area and the borrower may have been the owner of the property or a renter of the property affected.

HUD Provisions
Property Damaged Beyond Repair - Designated Major Catastrophe
Data Reference : HUD Release to Mortgage Lenders

Please note, the following guidelines has been obtained directly from HUD and included for illustrative purposes. Program availability, eligibility requirements, timelines, and other matters are subject to change at any time.

You should refer to the applicable HUD release to obtain the most up-to-date standards.

1.   Eligible Property -   The special DIL option may only be offered on property that meets the following criteria

      a.   The property is located within a Presidentially-Declared Major Disaster Area in Alabama, Florida, Louisiana, Mississippi and Texas approved for individual assistance, and the home has either;

      b.   suffered substantial damage attributable to Hurricanes Katrina, Rita or Wilma, or;

      c.   the cost of estimated storm damage repairs exceeds available hazard and flood insurance recoveries by the greater of $25,000 or 25%.

      Substantial damage is defined as homes with storm damage affecting more than 50 percent of the structure or with estimated repair costs that would exceed 50 percent of the home's pre-storm replacement value.

2.   Properties Outside Individual Assistance Areas – Mortgages secured by properties within a Presidentially-Declared Major Disaster Area in Alabama, Florida,

175

Louisiana, Mississippi and Texas approved for public assistance may also be eligible for the special DIL option if they meet all other requirements identified herein.

3. Borrowers - The special DIL option may be extended to individual borrowers, who have an FHA-insured mortgage on eligible property, cannot continue to occupy the home as a principal residence due to storm damage and have released available insurance recoveries and Community Development Block Grant funds for home repairs to the mortgagee for application to the mortgage debt.

4. PFS - Qualified properties do not have to be offered for sale through HUD's pre-foreclosure sale program (PFS) before acceptance of a deed-in-lieu as presently required under Mortgagee Letter 00-05, dated January 19, 2000. No justification for the failure to attempt a PFS is required.

5. Conveyance Property Condition – A mortgagee may accept a DIL on an eligible hurricane damaged property and convey the property to HUD without repairing the damage provided that all hazard and flood insurance claims are settled before the conveyance to the Secretary and, pursuant to provisions of 24 CFR 203.379(a)(1), the claim for insurance benefits is reduced by the Secretary's estimate of the cost of repairs or the insurance recovery received by the mortgagee, whichever is greater.

In accordance with regulation 24 CFR 203.378(d), this deduction for property damage repairs shall not exceed the amount of the FHA insurance benefit claim.

Standard DIL requirements that the borrower turn the property over to the mortgagee in broom clean condition, remove all personal property, and deliver keys and other fixtures to the mortgagee at time of conveyance are waived.

Prior to conveyance of an eligible damaged property, the mortgagee must send a written request for approval of the repair cost estimate to HUD's assigned Management & Marketing (M&M) Contractor along with documentation that the property meets the eligibility criteria of paragraph 1 for the special DIL option.

The request should identify the extent and cause of the damage and the amount of any insurance proceeds received or pending and include a copy of a contractor or insurer prepared estimate of the cost of repairing all damage caused by fire, flood, hurricane, earthquake, or tornado. Whenever available, the request must also include a copy of the insurer's settlement statement, which provides a breakdown of the insurance payment and lists, by item, labor costs, material costs, contractor overhead, and profit and the applied sales tax and tax percentage. The Contractor shall review the request and confirm HUD's estimate of the cost of repairing the damage no later than ten (10) calendar days following receipt.

6. Demolition Action – If a local government authority has recommended or required that the home be demolished because of substantial damage, significant structural deficiencies and/or the presence of a life threatening hazard and the mortgagee and the borrower agree that the home cannot be rebuilt, the building must be demolished prior to conveyance of the property to HUD.

Prior to demolition, the mortgagee must submit a written approval request to HUD's assigned Management & Marketing (M&M) Contractor as provided in paragraph 5 along with documentation supporting the determination that the home should be demolished. Supporting documentation must include a contractor prepared repair cost estimate and a copy of a letter or notice posted on the property by the unit of local government requiring the demolition. The notice may be described as a Notice of Unsafe Conditions, Notice of Imminent Danger to Collapse, Notice of Pending Demolition, or Notice of Condemnation. The M&M Contractor shall review the requests, confirm HUD's estimate of the repair cost and advise the mortgagee whether or not the proposed demolition action should be completed.

In instances where the mortgagee/mortgagor believes that the property should be demolished because of substantial damage, significant structural deficiencies and/or the presence of life threatening hazard, yet the unit of local government has not issued a letter or posted a notice due to the volume of properties damaged as a result of the hurricane, the mortgagees may still submit a request for approval of demolition or make a demolition recommendation. In that instance, the mortgagee must provide a detailed analysis to support the recommendation or demolition request in addition to the required repair cost estimate.

7. Claim Filing – In filing a Part A Claim for insurance benefits, the mortgagee must:

a. Describe the extent of the damage in the mortgagee comments section of Form HUD-27011, Part A;

b. Describe all coverage's under property insurance policies that were in place at the time of the disasters and the actions that were taken by the borrower and mortgagee to file and settle property insurance claims for hazard and flood damages and obtain recoveries for all covered losses;

c. Validate that all damage resulted from the hurricane(s) and/or hurricane related flooding and that the home is not habitable;

d. Enter in Part A, item 27, the greater of the hazard and flood insurance recoveries or the HUD approved estimate of the cost of repairs.

If the Part A claim is submitted before proceeds of the agreed insurance settlement is actually received, the mortgagee may use the anticipated recovery amount for purposes of determining the reduction from insurance benefits for the property damage as provided in subparagraph 7(d) above. When the proceeds are received, any necessary adjustment will be made on line 119 of Part B. If the actual proceeds received are less than expected, the mortgagee will be entitled to reimbursement of the difference between the expected proceeds amount and the proceeds actually received only if both are greater than the HUD approved estimate of damage repairs. If actual proceeds received are greater than anticipated, a Part B claim adjustment will be necessary only for the amount by which total recoveries exceed the amount previously credited on the Part A claim.

8. Financial Analysis – Mortgagees must normally obtain information and documentation necessary to assess the borrower's inability to continue to support the mortgage debt as provided in Mortgagee Letter 00-05, dated January 19, 2000. That evaluation is not required where the property has been damaged to the point that it is uninhabitable. Evidence of inhabitability should be documented in the servicing file.

9. Borrower Consideration - The borrower is entitled to consideration of $5,000 upon satisfaction of the requirements of the deed-in-lieu agreement if the property is vacant and clear title is provided. The mortgagee shall pay the borrower consideration and enter the payment amount on form HUD-27011, Single-Family Application for Insurance Benefits, Part D, item 305, Disbursements for HIP, taxes, ground rents, and water rates, eviction costs, and other disbursements not shown elsewhere. The description field for the payment should identify the qualifying disaster and clearly indicate how the funds were applied. All or part of this consideration may be applied as follows if approved by the borrower in the DIL agreement:

a. Toward discharge or discounted payoff of junior liens as necessary to clear the title.

b. Toward payoff of accrued foreclosure costs and other legal fees actually incurred by the mortgagee not to exceed the reimbursement guidelines specified by HUD in Mortgagee Letter 2005-30, dated July 12, 2005.

c. As a credit against uninsured property, repair costs that would normally be deducted from the claim for insurance benefits or the cost of an approved demolition if that expense were not otherwise covered by a local, state, or federal entity.

10. Claimable Expenses – Reimbursable expenses include title evidence costs, the consideration paid to (or on behalf of) the borrower, a $250 mortgagee incentive fee for administrative expenses and attorney fees not to exceed $400 for legal services in processing the DIL. The mortgagee may not include in its claim for insurance benefits any foreclosure or legal fees incurred prior to acceptance of the DIL.

11. Tax Consequences – Provisions of the Katrina Emergency Tax Relief Act of 2005 (Public Law 109-73, enacted September 23, 2005), provide relief from the potential federal income tax consequences of debt forgiveness to individuals whose principal residence on August 25, 2005 was located in core disaster areas for Hurricane Katrina only. All borrowers should be advised to obtain independent financial advice about tax consequences of the transaction before executing a DIL.

12. Credit Explanation Letters – The mortgagee shall, in addition to any monetary consideration provided to the borrower, provide the borrower with a credit explanation letter to alleviate potential adverse credit impacts from the DIL action in a format substantially similar to Attachment A.

13. Future Participation in FHA Programs – All borrowers who elect to convey property to HUD via deed in lieu of foreclosure under the special provisions described in this mortgagee letter shall be considered "non-occupants" under HUD property disposition rules and shall not be eligible to repurchase the same property. Subject to that restriction, they shall not be barred from immediate participation in FHA insured loan and property disposition programs because of the voluntary conveyance. A borrower shall not be ineligible for new FHA-insured financing because of a CAIVRS record of a deed-in-lieu claim paid pursuant to this special authority if a credit report

shows satisfactory credit prior to the disaster and any derogatory credit subsequent to that date can be related to the effects of the disaster. Mortgagees should refer to Mortgagee Letter 2006-01 dated January 9, 2006 for more specific FHA underwriting guidance to accommodate disaster victims.

Figure 9:2 - Data Reference : HUD Release to Mortgage Lenders

SAMPLE LETTER
DISASTER RELATED DIL
HUD RELEASE

[Prepare on mortgagee's letterhead and provide to borrower(s). Also, provide cover letter explaining that they may wish to send the letter below to credit reporting agencies or other parties that will be considering extending credit to the borrower(s).]

To Whom It May Concern:

Our records indicate that _____ was the mortgagor of record of an FHA-insured mortgage held by _____ on the property located at _____. The FHA Case Number was XXX-XXXXXX-XXX. The original principal balance on this mortgage was $_____, with an interest rate of XX%. The date of the first payment due on the mortgage was _____, with a term of _____ months.

As a result of (insert name of declared disaster), the property securing this loan was seriously damaged or destroyed. The damage made the home uninhabitable and it was not financially feasible to repair or rebuild the dwelling. The borrower worked with the mortgage holder to obtain all available hazard and flood insurance recoveries for application to the mortgage debt, voluntarily conveyed title to the property to _____ on _____ and was granted a release from all remaining financial obligations under the mortgage.

Due to the extreme circumstances resulting from (insert name of declared disaster), both (insert name of mortgagee) and the Department of Housing and Urban Development jointly request that any potential creditors take notice of these circumstances when deciding whether to grant credit to this borrower.

Figure 9:3 - Data Reference : HUD Release to Mortgage Lenders

Bankruptcy

If the homeowner files for bankruptcy protection, the loss mitigation process will alter. Upon receipt of notification that a homeowner has filed bankruptcy, the individual representing the mortgage lender will begin conducting the loss mitigation negotiation with the homeowner's attorney.

- Provide information to the homeowner's attorney relating to the availability of the loss mitigation options

- Provide detailed instruction regarding the documentation and actions necessary to facilitate the workout discussions

- Detail documentation requirements and remittal timeframes

- Provide contact information for the loss mitigation department

The processes of the loss mitigation negotiation will then continue according to the normal schedule, assessment action and negotiation elements. The variation is that the attorney will represent the homeowner in the negotiation process. All of the loss mitigation negotiations must be completed prior to the completion or discharge of the bankruptcy.

The final negotiation agreement will be submitted for review by the Bankruptcy Court before it is finalized and executed.

ATTORNEY FEES
Data Reference : HUD Release to Mortgage Lenders

Please note, the following guidelines has been obtained directly from HUD and included for illustrative purposes. Program availability, eligibility requirements, timelines, and other matters are subject to change at any time.

You should refer to the applicable HUD release to obtain the most up-to-date standards.

HUD has established attorney fees that are reasonable for actions relating to various loss mitigation workouts. These fees considered reasonable vary depending on the State of the loss mitigation action. The following chart illustrates the attorney fees that are conspired reasonable according to the established HUD Guidelines.

HUD SCHEDULE OF STANDARD ATTORNEY'S FEES
COPYRIGHT HUD

State	Non-Judicial Foreclosure	Judicial Foreclosure	Bankruptcy	Possession Action	DIL
AK	1,000	----	750	350	250
AL	500	----	750	350	300
AR	500	750	750	250	250
AZ	500	500	750	250	200
CA	600		750	500	250
CO	700		750	250	200
CT	----	750	750	350	275
DC	500	----	750	350	300
DE	----		750	300	275
FL	----		750	350	300
GA	500	----	750	350	300
GU	1,200	----	750	350	250
HI	----		750	350	250
IA	500		750	300	250
ID	400	----	750	350	250
IL	----		750	300	250
IN	----	750	750	300	250
KS	----	750	750	300	200
KY	----	750	750	350	300
LA	----	750	750	300	200
MA	----		750	600	275
MD	750	----	750	350	300
ME	----		750	500	275
MI	500		750	300	250

Figure 9:5 - Data Reference : HUD Release to Mortgage Lenders

State	Non-Judicial Foreclosure	Judicial Foreclosure	Bankruptcy	Possession Action	DIL
MN	500		750	300	250
MO	550		750	300	200
MS	500	----	750	350	300
MT	575	----	750	350	250
NC	500	----	750	350	300
ND	----		750	300	250
NE	500	750	750	300	250
NH	750		750	400	275
NJ	----		750	350	275
NM	----		750	250	200
NV	550	----	750	350	250
NY	750		750	700	275
OH	----		750	300	250
OK	----		750	250	200
OR	550	----	750	350	250
PA	----		750	400	275
PR	----		750	275	275
RI	600	----	750	500	275
SC	----	750	750	350	300
SD	500		750	300	250
TN	500	----	750	350	300
TX	450	----	750	300	200
UT	425		750	250	200
VA	500	----	750	350	300
VI	----		750	275	275
VT	----		750	350	275
WA	550	----	750	350	250
WI	----		750	300	250
WV	500	----	750	350	300
WY	600	----	750	350	250

Figure 9:6 - Data Reference : HUD Release to Mortgage Lenders

Appendix A
Glossary of Terms

1-year ARM: An adjustable-rate mortgage (ARM) that has an initial interest rate for one year, and thereafter has an adjustment interval of one year. The adjustment is based on comparison interest caps and the indexed rate

3/1 ARM: An adjustable-rate mortgage (ARM) that has an initial interest rate for three years, and thereafter has an adjustment interval of one year. The adjustment is based on comparison interest caps and the indexed rate.

5/1 ARM: An adjustable-rate mortgage (ARM) that has an initial interest rate for five years, and thereafter has an adjustment interval of one year. The adjustment is based on comparison interest caps and the indexed rate

7/1 ARM: An adjustable-rate mortgage (ARM) that has an initial interest rate for seven years, and thereafter has an adjustment interval of one year. The adjustment is based on comparison interest caps and the indexed rate

10/1 ARM: An adjustable-rate mortgage (ARM) that has an initial interest rate for ten years, and thereafter has an adjustment interval of one year. The adjustment is based on comparison interest caps and the indexed rate

Abstract of Title: A written history of all the transactions that bear on the title to a specific piece of land An abstract of title covers the time from when the property was first sold to the present. Used by the Title Company to produce a title binder

Acceleration Clause: The section of a mortgage document that allows the lender to speed up the payment date in the event of default, making the entire principal amount due

Acre: An area of land 43.560 square feet

Adjustable Rate Mortgage: Mortgage in which the rate of interest is adjusted based on a standard rate index. Most ARM's have caps on how much the interest rate may increase

Adjustment Interval: How often the loan's rate can be changed

Alternative Mortgage: 7/23 and 5/25 mortgages with a one-time rate adjustment after seven years and five years respectively Also known as a hybrid mortgage or a two-step mortgage

Amortization Schedule: A timetable for the gradual repayment of a mortgage loan An amortization schedule indicates the amount of each payment applied to interest and principal, and the remaining balance after each payment is made

Amortization Term: The amount of time required to amortize (repay) a mortgage loan. The amortization term is usually expressed in months. A 30-year fixed rate mortgage, for example, has an amortization term of 360 months

Annual Percentage Rate (APR): A standardized method of calculating the cost of a mortgage, stated as a yearly rate which includes such items as interest, mortgage insurance, and certain points or credit costs

Appraisal: A written report by a qualified appraiser estimating the value of the property

Appraised Value: An opinion of a property's fair market value, based on an appraiser's inspection and analysis of the property

Appraiser: A person qualified by education, training, and experience to estimate the value of real property

Appreciation: An increase in the value of a property due to changes in market conditions or improvements to the property

ARM: See Adjustable Rate Mortgage

Assessed Value: The value of a property as determined by a public tax assessor for the purpose of taxation

Assumable: A mortgage that a buyer can assume, or take over, from the seller of the property

Balloon Mortgage: A loan that has regular monthly payments, which amortize over a stated term but call for a final lump sum (balloon payment) at the end of a specified term, or maturity date such as 10 years

Basis Points: 1/100th of 1 percent If an interest rate changes 50 basis points, for example, it has move ½ of 1 percent

Binder: See title binder

Biweekly Mortgage: A mortgage that schedules payments every two weeks instead of the standard monthly payment The 26 biweekly payments are each equal to one-half of the monthly payment. The result for the homeowner is a substantial reduction in interest payments because the mortgage is paid off sooner. See also prepayment plan

Bridge loan: A loan that "bridges" the gap between the purchase of a new home and the sale of the homeowner's current home. The homeowner's current home is used as collateral and the money is used to close on the new home before the current home is sold. Some are structured so they completely pay off the old home's first mortgage at the bridge loan's closing. Others pile the new debt on top of the old. They usually run for a term of six months

Broker: See mortgage broker

Broker Premium: A premium paid to the mortgage broker as the "middleman" in the mortgage process between the lender and the homeowner
Built-ins: Cabinets, ranges, ceiling fans and other items permanently attached to the structure, and which a buyer may assume will remain with the structure

Buy down: The process of trading money for a lower mortgage rate. The homeowner "buys down" the interest rate on a mortgage by paying discount points up front. It can also be a mortgage in which an initial lump sum payment is made to reduce a homeowner's monthly payments during the first few years of a mortgage

Caps: The maximum amount the interest rate can change annually or cumulatively over the life of an adjustable rate mortgage. F or example, if the caps are 2 percent annual and 6 percent life of loan, a mortgage with a first-year rate of 10 percent could rise to no more than 12 percent the second year, and no more than 16 percent over the entire life of the loan

Certificate of Title: A statement provided by the Title Company or attorney stating that the title to the real estate is legally held by the current owner

Chattel: Personal property

Clear title: A title that is free of liens or legal questions as to ownership of a piece of property

Closing: The meeting at which the sale of a property is finalized The buyer signs the lender agreement for the mortgage and pays' closing costs and escrow amounts. The buyer and seller sign documents to transfer the ownership of the property. Also known as the settlement

Closing costs: Expenses incurred by buyers and sellers in transferring ownership of a property. Closing costs normally include an origination fee, an attorney's fee, taxes, escrow payments, and charges for title insurance. Lenders or Real Estate Agents provide estimates of closing costs to prospective homebuyers

Closing Statement: A financial disclosure accounting for all funds changing hands at the closing See also HUD-1 Statement

Cloud on title: Any fact or condition that could adversely affect the title

Commission: In real estate, the broker, or mortgage associates fee for assisting in the transaction Usually expressed as a percentage of the total paid by the buyer

Commitment: A formal offer by a lender stating the approved terms for lending money to a homebuyer

Common Area Assessment: A levy against individual unit owners in a condominium or planned unit development to pay for upkeep, repairs, and improvements to the property's common areas, such as corridors, elevators, parking lots, swimming pools and tennis courts

Comparables: Refers to "comparable properties" which are used for comparative purposes in the appraisal process.

Comps are recently sold properties that are similar in size, location, and amenities to the home for sale. Comps help an appraiser determine the fair market value of a property

Condominium: A real estate project in which each unit owner has title to a unit of the project, and sometimes and undivided interest in the common areas

Conforming Loan: A loan that conforms to the standard rules for purchase by Freddie Mac or Fannie Mae

Contingency: A condition that must be met before a contract is legally binding. For example, homebuyers often include a contingency that specifies that the contract is not binding until after a satisfactory report from a home inspector

Contract: In real estate parlance, the contract is the legal document by which buyer and seller make offers and counteroffers. The real estate contract describes the property, includes or excludes items in the property, names the price, apportions the closing costs between the parties and sets forth a closing date. When a buyer and seller agree on the terms and sign the same document the property is said to be "under contract". More formally known as the agreement for the sale, purchase agreement, or earnest money contract

Conventional Mortgage: Usually refers to a fixed-rate, 30-year mortgage that is not insured by FHA, Farmers Home Administration, or Veterans Administration

Convertible Mortgage: An adjustable rate mortgage ARM that can be converted to a fixed mortgage under specific conditions

Cooperative: A type of multiple ownership in which the residents of a multiunit housing complex own shares in the cooperative corporation that owns the property, giving each resident the right to occupy a specific apartment or unit

Cost-of-funds: A yield index based upon the cost of funds to savings & loan institution in the San Francisco Federal Home Loan Bank District. It is one of the indexes commonly used to set the rate of adjustable rate mortgages

Covenant: A written restriction on the use of land, most commonly in use today in homeowners associations

Credit report: A report on a person's credit history prepared by a credit bureau and used by a lender in

determining a loan applicant's record for paying debts in a timely manner

Debt-to-Income Ratio: The percentage of a person's monthly earnings used to pay off all debt obligations Lenders consider two ratios, constructed in slightly different ways. The first called the front-end ratio, the ratio of the monthly housing expenses – including principal, interest, property taxes, and insurance, (PITI) is compared to the homeowner's gross, pretax monthly income. In the back-end ratio, a homeowner's other debts such as auto loans and credit cards are figured in. Lenders usually consider both and set an acceptable ratio. Some lenders and some lending qualifying agencies only consider the back-end ratio

Deed: The legal document conveying title to the property

Depreciation: A decline in the value of a property as opposed to appreciation

Discount Points: A type of point (1 percent of the loan) paid by the homeowner to reduce the interest rate

Down payment: The amount of a property's purchase price that the buyer pays in cash and does not finance with a mortgage

Earnest money: A deposit made by potential homebuyers during negotiations with the seller. The sum shows a seller that the buyer is serious about purchasing a property

Easement: The right of another to use a property The most common easements are for utility lines

80-10-10 Loan: A combination of an 80 percent loan-to-value first mortgage, a 10 percent down payment and a 10 percent home equity loan. This is also sometimes referred to as a CLTV (Combined Loan-to-Value)

Encumbrance: A lien, charge or liability against a property

Equal Credit: A federal law that requires lenders and other creditors to make credit equally available with out discrimination based on race, color, religion, national origin, age, sex, marital status, or receipt of income from public assistance programs

Equity: The value of a homeowner's unencumbered interest in real estate Equity is the difference between the homes fair market value and the unpaid balance of the mortgage and any outstanding liens Equity increases as the mortgage is paid down or as the property enjoys appreciation

Escrow Payment: The portion of a homeowner's monthly mortgage payment that is held by the loan servicer to pay for taxes and insurance Also known as reserves The loan servicer holds the escrow funds separately from money meant to pay principal and interest

Fair Credit Reporting Act: A consumer protection law that regulates the disclosure of consumer credit reports by credit reporting agencies and establishes procedures for correcting mistakes on a person's credit record

Fannie Mae: Nickname for Federal National Mortgage Association It is a government-chartered non-bank financial services company and the nation's largest source of financing for home mortgages It was started to make sure mortgage money is available in all areas of the country

FHA Mortgage: A mortgage insured by the Federal Housing Administration

First mortgage: A mortgage that is the primary lien against a property

Fixed-rate Mortgage: A mortgage in which the interest rate does not change during the entire term of the loan, most often 15 or 30 years

Flood Insurance: Insurance that compensates for the physical property damage resulting from rising water It is required for properties located in federally designated flood areas

Foreclosure: The legal process by which a homeowner in default on a mortgage is deprived of interest in the property This usually involves a forced sale of the property at public auction with the proceeds of the sale being applied to the mortgage debt

Freddie Mac: Nickname for Federal Home Loan Mortgage Corp A financial corporation chartered by the federal government to buy pools of mortgages from lenders and sell securities backed by these mortgages

Ginnie Mae: Nickname for the Government National Mortgage Association

Good Faith Estimate: A written estimate of closing costs that the lender must provide to prospective homebuyers within three days of submitting a mortgage loan application

Government National Mortgage Association (Ginnie Mae) A government-owned corporation within the US Department of Housing and Urban Development (HUD) Created by Congress in 1968, GNMA has responsibility for the special assistance loan program known as Ginnie Mae

Hazard Insurance: Insurance coverage that compensates for physical damage to property from natural disasters such as fire and other hazards Depending on where a piece of property is located, lenders may also require flood insurance or policies covering windstorms (hurricanes) or earthquakes

Home Inspection: An inspection by a building professional that evaluates the structural and mechanical condition of a property

Homeowners Association: A nonprofit association that manages the common areas of a condominium or PUD Unit owners pays the association a fee to maintain areas owned jointly

Homeowner's Insurance: An insurance policy that combines personal liability insurance and hazard insurance coverage for a residence and its contents

Housing Expense: The percentage of gross monthly income that goes toward paying a Ratio mortgage or rent on a home

HUD-1: The document with an itemized listing of closing costs payable at the closing or settlement meeting when buying property The closing costs can include a commission, loan fees, and points, and sums set aside for escrow payments, taxes, and insurance. It is signed by both the buyer and the seller, who may be paying some of the closing costs. The statement form is published by HUD

Hybrid Mortgage: See alternative mortgage products.

Index: A published measure of the cost of money that lenders use to calculate the rate on an ARM The most common indexes are the one-year Treasury Constant Maturity Yield and the FHLB 11th District Cost of Funds

Indexed Rate: The sum of the published index plus the margin For example, if the index were 9 percent and the margin 2.75 percent, the indexed rate would be 11.75 percent. Often, lenders charge less than the indexed rate the first year of an ARM

Initial Interest Rate: Starting rate of an ARM

Interest Tax Deduction: Most mortgage holders can deduct all the interest paid on the loan in filing income tax The deduction applies to people with just on mortgage on a primary residence, as well as those with a combination of loans. Within certain time limits set by the IRS, points paid up front on a mortgage are usually deductible in the year the house was purchased

Jumbo Mortgage: Mortgages larger than the limits set by Fannie Mae and Freddie Mac. A jumbo mortgage will carry a higher interest rate than a conventional mortgage

Lease-purchase: A financing option that allows a potential homebuyer to lease a property with the option to buy Often constructed so the monthly rent payment covers the owner's first mortgage payment, plus an additional amount as a savings deposit to accumulate cash for a down payment A seller may agree to a lease-purchase option if the housing market is saturated and the seller is having a difficult time selling the property

Lien: A legal hold or claim from one person on the property of another The lien placed by a first mortgage is special. It is called a first lien and takes precedence over others

Lifetime Rate Cap: In an ARM, it limits the amount that the interest rate can increase or decrease over the life of the loan. See also caps

Lis Pendens: A pending lawsuit; in real estate, the constructive notice filed in public records that a legal dispute exists over a piece of property

Livery of Seizen: Under common law, the process of transferring title

Loan Origination: The process by which a mortgage lender obtains a mortgage secured by real property An origination fee is charged by the lender to process all forms involved in obtaining a mortgage

Loan-to-value (LTV) Ratio: The ratio of a mortgage loan amount to the property's appraised value or selling price, whichever is less For example, if a home is sold for $100,000 and the mortgage amount is $80,000 the LTV is 80%

Lock: Lender's guarantee that the mortgage rate quoted will be good for a specific amount of time. The homebuyer usually wants the lock to stay in effect until the date of the closing

Lock-and-Float: Rate programs offered by companies that allow homeowners to lock in the current interest rate on a mortgage for a specified period, while also letting them "float" the rate down if market conditions improve before closing

Low-down Mortgages: Mortgages with a low down payment, usually less than 10 percent. Frannie Mae and Freddie Mac design loan programs that spell out a set of standards for lenders. In recent years, these government-chartered agencies have made low-down mortgages more available

Margin: The number of percentage points added to the index on a one-year ARM

Maturity: The date on which the principal balance of a loan becomes due and payable

Mortgage: A legal document that uses property as collateral to secure payment of a debt

Mortgage Banker: The lender that originates a mortgage loan, the one making the loan directly and closing the loan

Mortgage Broker: An individual or company that brings homeowners and lenders together for the purpose of loan origination Unlike a mortgage banker, brokers do not fund the loan but work on behalf of several lenders. Brokers typically require a fee or a commission for their service See broker premium

Mortgage Insurance: A policy that insures the lender against loss should the homeowner default on a mortgage. Depending on the loan, the insurance can be issued by government agencies such as the FHA or a private company. It is part of the monthly mortgage payment. (See also private mortgage insurance PMI)

Negative Amortization: A gradual increase in mortgage debt that happens when a monthly payment does not cover the entire principal and interest due The shortfall is added to the remaining balance to create "negative" amortization

No-doc or low-doc Loan: These no-documentation or low-documentation loans are designed for the entrepreneur or self-employed, for recent immigrants with money in foreign countries or for homeowners who cannot or choose not to reveal information about their incomes

Note: The document giving evidence of mortgage indebtedness, including the amount and terms of repayment

Origination Fee: A fee paid to the lender for processing a loan application

Owner financing A transaction in which the seller of a house provides all or part of the financing Sellers may provide financing because they need to sell the property right away or they are having difficulty selling the house and want to provide financing as an incentive to a buyer
Periodic rate cap: In an ARM, it limits how much an interest rate can increase or decrease during any one-adjustment period See also caps

PITI: Stands for principal, interest, taxes and insurance that are the usual components of a monthly mortgage payment

PITI Reserves: A cash amount that a homebuyer must have on hand after making a down payment and paying all closing costs. The reserves required by a lender must equal the amount a buyer would pay for PITI for a specific number of months

Plat: A map that shows a parcel of land and how it is subdivided into individual lots Plat maps also show the locations of streets and easements

PMI: See private mortgage insurance

Points: A point equals 1 percent of a mortgage loan. Lenders charge points as a way to make a profit. Homeowners may pay discount points to reduce the loan interest rate. Buyers are prohibited from paying points on HUD or VA guaranteed loans

Pre-approval: This process goes a step further than pre-qualification. It means the lender has contacted the homeowner's employer, bank, and other places to verify all claims of earnings and assets. In return, the homeowner receives a letter stating the lender is willing to grant a mortgage for a specific amount within a limited period with the stipulation that there are no material changes to the homeowner's situation

Prepayment Penalty: A fee imposed by certain lenders if the first mortgage is paid off early

Prepayment Plan: Similar to biweekly mortgage, but operated by a third party In it, the homeowner pays to the third party, half the monthly mortgage payment every two weeks At the end of the year, the plan operators typically take the extra money that results from the process and sends lump sum payment to the participants' lenders

Pre-qualification: An early evaluation by a lender of a potential homebuyer's credit report, plus earnings, savings, and debt information The homebuyer gets a non-binding estimate of the mortgage amount the homeowner would qualify for, or how much house the homeowner can afford. Buyers who pre-qualify can go a step further and seek a pre-approval

Rate Lock: A commitment issued by a lender to the homebuyer or the mortgage broker guaranteeing a specific interest rate for a specified amount of time See also lock

Real Estate Agent: A person licensed to negotiate and transact the sale of real estate on behalf of the property owner

RESPA: Real Estate Settlement Procedures Act. A consumer protection law that requires lenders to give homebuyers advance notice of closing costs, which are payable at the closing or settlement meeting

Realtor: A real estate broker or an associate who holds an active membership in a local real estate board that is affiliated with the National Association of Realtors

Refinancing: Securing a new loan in order to pay off the existing mortgage or to gain access to the existing equity in the home

Roll-in Loan: A refinance loan that rolls any closing costs or fees into the loan. These programs best serve people who have a reasonable amount of equity, want to reduce their overall interest expense, and plan to stay in their homes

Rural Housing Service (RHS): The agency in the US Department of Agriculture providing financing to farmers and other qualified homeowners buying property in rural areas who are unable to obtain loans elsewhere. It offers low-interest-rate loans with no down payment to homeowners with low-to-moderate incomes who live in rural areas or small towns

Sales Agreement: A written contract signed by the buyer and the seller of a house stating the terms and conditions under which the property will be sold

Second Mortgage: A mortgage on the property that has a lien position behind the first mortgage

Servicer: An organization that collects monthly mortgage principal and interest payments from homeowners and manages escrow accounts for paying taxes and homeowners' insurance premiums The servicer often services mortgages that have been purchased by an investor in the secondary mortgage market

Settlement: See closing

Sub-prime Mortgage: A mortgage granted to a homeowner considered sub-prime, that is, a person with a less-than perfect credit report. Sub-prime homeowners either have missed payments on a debt or have been late with payments. Lenders charge a higher interest rate to compensate for potential losses from customers who may run into trouble and default

Time is of the Essence: A phrase inserted in contracts to require a punctual performance

Title: A legal document proving a person's right to claim entitlement to a property, including the history of the property's ownership

Title Binder: Written evidence of temporary title insurance coverage

Title Company: A company that specializes in examining and insuring titles to real estate

Title insurance: Insurance that protects against loss from disputes over ownership of a property. A policy may protect the mortgage lender and/or the homebuyer

Title search: A check of title records to ensure that the seller is the legal owner of a property and that there are no liens or other claims against the property

Transfer Tax: State or local tax levied when title passes from one owner to another

Treasury Index: An index used to determine interest rate changes for certain ARM mortgages. It is based on the results of auctions that the US Treasury holds for its Treasury bills and securities or is derived from the US Treasury's daily yield curve, which is based on the closing market bid yields on actively traded Treasury securities in the over-the-counter market

Truth-in-Lending Act (TILA): A federal law that requires lenders to disclose, in writing, the terms and conditions of a mortgage, including the annual percentage rate APR and other charges

Underwriter: A company or person undertaking the responsibility for issuing a mortgage. Underwriters analyze a homeowner's credit worthiness and set the loan amount

VA Mortgage: A loan backed by the Veterans Administration. It requires very low or no down payments and has less stringent requirements for qualification. Members of the US armed forces are eligible for the loans under certain qualifying conditions

Wraparound Mortgage: A new mortgage that includes the remaining balance on the old mortgage plus a new amount

FORECLOSURE PREVENTION

Loss Mitigation Specialist
Table of Contents

DEBT-TO-INCOME RATIO EXERCISES

To calculate a borrower's debt to income take the total monthly debt load and divide it by the total monthly income. For example:

A borrower who earns $2800.00 monthly and has installment debt of $750.00 monthly has a debt-to-income ratio of 26.78%.

D   I   R

750 / 2800 = 26.78%

1.	Income $6200	
	Debt $1900	
	Ratio _____ %	

2.	Income $3000
	Debt $1350
	Ratio _____ %

3.	Income $3750
	Debt $ 970
	Ratio _____ %

4.	Income $1600
	Debt $ 340
	Ratio _____ %

5.	Income $2000
	Debt $ 420
	Ratio _____ %

6.	Income $2480
	Debt $ 920
	Ratio _____ %

7.	Income $4200
	Debt $1850
	Ratio _____ %

8.	Income $4800
	Debt $2175
	Ratio _____ %

9.	Income $5100
	Debt $1950
	Ratio _____ %

10.	Income $5500
	Debt $1775
	Ratio _____ %

11.	Income $5750
	Debt $1900
	Ratio _____ %

12.	Income $3425
	Debt $1350
	Ratio _____ %

13.	Income $4387
	Debt $1218
	Ratio _____ %

14.	Income $2330
	Debt $ 961
	Ratio _____ %

Kenney

POST-FOREBEARANCE PAYMENT

Use the mortgage payment to calculate the forebearance payment that requires the homeowner to repay arrearages at ½ times the regularly stipulated payment.

Mortgage	+	½ Mortgage	=	Post-Forebearance Payment
$750	+	$375	=	$1126

1. Mortgage Repayment $1900

2. Mortgage Repayment $1350

3. Mortgage Repayment $970

4. Mortgage Repayment $340

5. Mortgage Repayment $420

6. Mortgage Repayment $920

7. Mortgage Repayment $1850

8. Mortgage Repayment $2175

9. Mortgage Repayment $1950

10. Mortgage Repayment $1775

11. Mortgage Repayment $1200

12. Mortgage Repayment $1650

13. Mortgage Repayment $1218

14. Mortgage Repayment $961

POST-FOREBEARANCE PAYMENT

Use the mortgage payment and post forbearance arrearages payment to calculate the potential post forbearance front end DTI.

Mortgage	+	½ Mortgage	=	Post-Forebearance Payment
$750	+	$375	=	$1126

Total Payment	/	Income	=	Repayment Ratio
$750	/	$2800 =		26.78%

1.
Mortgage	$1900
Repayment	+
Income	$6200
Ratio	%

2.
Mortgage	$1350
Repayment	+
Income	$5000
Ratio	%

3.
Mortgage	$970
Repayment	+
Income	$3750
Ratio	%

4.
Mortgage	$340
Repayment	+
Income	$1600
Ratio	%

5.
Mortgage	$420
Repayment	+
Income	$2000
Ratio	%

6.
Mortgage	$920
Repayment	+
Income	$2480
Ratio	%

7.
Mortgage	$1850
Repayment	+
Income	$4200
Ratio	%

8.
Mortgage	$2175
Repayment	+
Income	$4800
Ratio	%

9.
Mortgage	$1950
Repayment	+
Income	$5100
Ratio	%

10.
Mortgage	$1775
Repayment	+
Income	$5500
Ratio	%

11.
Mortgage	$1900
Repayment	+
Income	$5750
Ratio	%

12.
Mortgage	$1350
Repayment	+
Income	$3425
Ratio	%

BACK-END DEBT

Calculate the back end debt ratio.

Mortgage	+	Monthly Payment=		Debt Load	
$900	+	$300		=	$200

Debt Load	/	Income		=	DTI
$1200	/	$3000		=	40%

1.
Mortgage	$1900
+ Other Debt	$1300

/ Income	$5700
= Ratio	

2.
Mortgage	$ 800
+ Other Debt	$ 556

/ Income	$3150
= Ratio	

3.
Mortgage	$ 428
+ Other Debt	$ 220

/ Income	$1670
= Ratio	

4.
Mortgage	$ 556
+ Other Debt	$ 353

/ Income	$2800
= Ratio	

5.
Mortgage	$2850
+ Other Debt	$1200

/ Income	$7500
= Ratio	

6.
Mortgage	$1155
+ Other Debt	$ 875

/ Income	$4800
= Ratio	

7.
Mortgage	$2100
+ Other Debt	$1100

/ Income	$6000
= Ratio	

8.
Mortgage	$ 510
+ Other Debt	$285

/ Income	$2250
= Ratio	

9.
Mortgage	$ 800
+ Other Debt	$200

/ Income	$3890
= Ratio	

10.
Mortgage	$1255
+ Other Debt	$1060

/ Income	$5575
= Ratio	

MODIFICATION CALCULATION

Calculate the payment difference for each of the rate modifications in the chart.

Loan Amount	Interest Rate 10.375 30-year Amortization	Interest Rate 6.250 30-year Amortization	Payment Difference
$100,000	$ 905.41	$ 614.72	
$125,000	$1131.76	$ 769.65	
$150.000	$1358.11	$ 923.58	
$175,000	$1584.76	$1077.51	
$200,000	$1810.81	$1231.43	
$225,000	$2037.17	$1385.36	

Kenney

Calculate the old and new Front End Ratio

Income	Interest Rate 10.375 30-year Amortization	Pre-Modification DTI	Interest Rate 6.250 30-year Amortization	Post-Modification DTI
$4175	$ 905.41		$ 614.72	
$4175	$1131.76		$ 769.65	
$4175	$1358.11		$ 923.58	
$7200	$1584.76		$1077.51	
$7200	$1810.81		$1231.43	
$$7200	$2037.17		$1385.36	

SAMPLE RATE SHEET

Grade	LTV	40 Year Fixed		30 Year Fixed	
		Par	<1.00>	Par	<1.00>
A 660+	97%	6.500	7.000	7.000	7.500
Mortgage 0X30	95%	6.125	6.625	6.500	7.000
Consumer 1X30	90%	6.000	6.500	6.125	6.625
BK/For 3/3	85%	5.875	6.125	6.000	6.500
DTI 41%	80%	5.750	6.250	5.875	6.375
	75%	5.625	6.125	5.750	6.250
B	95%	7.125	7.500	8.000	8.500
620-669	90%	7.000	7.375	7.875	8.375
Mtg 1x30	85%	6.625	7.000	7.500	8.000
Con any	80%	6.500	6.875	7.125	7.625
BK / For 3/3	75%	6.125	6.500	6.875	7.375
DTI 45%	70%	5.875	6.125	6.500	7.000
C	90%	7.500	8.000	8.500	
590-619	85%	7.375	7.875	8.375	
Mtg 2X60	80%	7.000	7.500	8.000	
Con any	75%	6.875	7.125	7.875	8.125
BK / For 2/2	70%	6.500	6.875	7.500	7.875
DTI 47%					
D	85%	7.875	8.375		
560-589	80%	7.500	8.000	8.500	
Mtg 90+	75%	7.125	7.625	8.375	
Con any	70%	6.875	7.125	8.250	
BK/ For 2/2					
DTI 50%					

www.ingramcontent.com/pod-product-compliance
Lightning Source LLC
Chambersburg PA
CBHW080422270326
41929CB00018B/3121